ELIZABETH R

ELIZABETH

R

The Role of the Monarchy Today

Antony Jay

With specially commissioned photographs
by David Secombe

BCA

LONDON · NEW YORK · SYDNEY · TORONTO

This edition published 1992 by
BCA by
arrangement with BBC Books,
a division of BBC Enterprises Limited,
Woodlands, 80 Wood Lane, London W12 0TT

First published 1992
© Crown Copyright 1992
CN 3476

Edited by Alex MacCormick
Text research by Sallyann Kleibel
Picture research by Paul Snelgrove
Designed by Tim Higgins
Set in Monotype Lasercomp Baskerville 169 by Butler & Tanner Ltd, Frome and London
Printed and bound in Great Britain by Butler & Tanner Ltd, Frome and London
Colour separations by Technik Ltd, Berkhamsted
Jacket printed by Belmont Press Ltd, Northampton

PAGE 1 A mounted bandsman of the Household Cavalry,
Windsor Castle, 1991.
PAGE 2 The Queen at the Royal Military Academy,
Sandhurst, in April 1991.

CONTENTS

INTRODUCTION

When Queen Elizabeth II came to the throne on 6 February 1952, Winston Churchill was Prime Minister and Harry S. Truman was the American President. In Britain tea, sugar, butter, cooking fats and sweets were still rationed. The new cinema releases of 1952 included *The Lavender Hill Mob, High Noon* and *Singing in the Rain*. The bank rate was raised from 2% to 4%. There were no motorways, computers, supermarkets or frozen food. It was the first year in which sales of television sets overtook radios, though there was only one (black and white) channel. The BBC was the only broadcasting authority. There was no hi-fi, no video and no colour supplements. Most of today's British citizens were not yet born.

ABOVE The coronation, 2 June 1953. There was only one (BBC) television channel broadcasting in black and white to fewer than a million homes. It was the outside broadcast of the coronation which started the surge in the popularity of television. Today there are over eighteen million television sets in Britain.

OPPOSITE The twenty-six-year-old Queen photographed by Baron in 1953. The war had been over less than eight years; sweets, sugar, butter and cooking fats were still rationed. Most of today's British citizens had not been born.

The Queen today, watching the news on television in the Palace of Holyroodhouse, Scotland. At the age of sixty-five she has now been doing the same job without a break for forty years.

Forty years later the world has changed a great deal, but the Queen's job has changed less than most. She still opens Parliament, presides over the Privy Council, receives state visitors, gives a weekly audience to the Prime Minister, takes the Trooping the Colour ceremony, entertains the diplomatic corps, accepts ambassadors' credentials, confers honours, opens hospitals, launches ships, and signs Acts of Parliament as she has done for the past forty years.

The Queen's activities are widely reported and well known, so well known in fact that we do not often stop to ask what they are intended to achieve or whether there is much more to the job of sovereign than providing colourful pageantry and a constitutional rubber stamp. The purpose of this book is to try and answer such questions. It looks at incidents in the fortieth year of the Queen's reign to see something of the work involved in supporting the monarchy and to examine what the monarchy is trying to achieve through its various activities. There are, after all, some 260 people employed full time in Buckingham Palace. Their whole working life is focused on helping the Queen do her job effectively. By looking at different aspects of that job over the year we can get an insight into how the institution of British monarchy goes about achieving its aims.

The job of the British monarchy is in fact two jobs: Head of the State and Head of the Nation. The first four chapters look at the first job, the formal, constitutional role of the sovereign: first 'inwards', in relation to the government of Britain, and then 'outwards', representing Britain to the rest of the world. The next five chapters look at the less clearly defined role of Head of the Nation, where the monarchy acts through social influence rather than constitutional authority – the honours system, garden parties, visits around the country, walkabouts, patronage, personal contact and relationship with the media. The final chapter summarises the functions the monarchy performs and the qualities the British people expect of it.

1

POMP AND CIRCUMSTANCE

At 11 a.m. on Wednesday 7 November 1990 the Earl of Airlie and Mr David Lightbown, MP for Staffordshire South-East, sat in the Equerry's Room in Buckingham Palace watching television and drinking coffee.

There was a traffic jam in the West End of London. The whole of Victoria had ground to a halt and there were long tailbacks around Vauxhall Cross and Hyde Park Corner.

Portcullis Pursuivant was in his place behind Rouge Croix Pursuivant and in front of Beaumont Herald Extraordinary. Bluemantle Pursuivant was on his left. Behind them were Somerset Herald, Windsor Herald, York Herald, Richmond Herald, Lancaster Herald in a procession that reads like a string of English provincial newspapers.

It was, of course, the annual State Opening of Parliament. The heralds play a major part because the College of Arms organizes the procession. The traffic jams form because a square mile of roads north of Westminster is cordoned off from 9.30 a.m. to 1 p.m. The Earl of Airlie is in the Equerry's Room drinking coffee because, as Lord Chamberlain of the Queen's House-

ABOVE The Queen and Prince Philip entering the House of Commons for the State Opening of Parliament in November 1990.

The imperial state crown goes to Parliament in a coach of its own.
Next day it is returned to the Jewel House in the Tower of London.
The crown is remodelled for each new sovereign.
OVERLEAF The Queen in the Irish state coach on her way to open
Parliament in November 1990. Parliament provides Buckingham
Palace with an MP as hostage for the Queen's safe return.

hold, it is his job to guard the Palace while the Queen is away, and David
Lightbown is with him because the Commons have to deliver one of their
members as a hostage for the safe return of the sovereign. He is chosen
because he is Vice Chamberlain of the Household, which actually means he
is one of the Government Whips.

A small part of the occasion is familiar from the television broadcast: the
Queen's journey from the Palace to Parliament in the Irish state coach drawn
by four Windsor Greys; Black Rod having the door of the chamber of the
Commons slammed in his face on the orders of the Serjeant-at-Arms; the
hammering on the door, followed by the representatives of the Commons in
cross-party pairs proceeding to the House of Lords; the Queen sitting on the
throne reading the 'Gracious Speech' outlining the government's legislative
programme for the coming session of Parliament. But, behind the few seconds
of pageantry which we watch on the television news, there are weeks of

The maces for the Serjeants-at-Arms. The regalia have
their own mounted escort and are saluted by the troops
along the route.

planning, preparation and rehearsal by hundreds of people. Horses are
groomed, soldiers are drilled, jewels are polished, streets are closed, traffic is
diverted, robes are cleaned, journeys are timed, fanfares are rehearsed, the
building is searched – ritually by the Yeomen of the Guard because of the
Gunpowder Plot in 1605 and in grim earnest by the security forces because
of present-day terrorism – the procession is marshalled, and the timing is
planned and rehearsed with such precision that it will not occur to spectators
that timing has been planned and rehearsed.

But suppose it did not happen. Suppose that for one reason or another the
whole ceremony had to be cancelled. How far would the functioning of
government in the United Kingdom be impaired or impeded? The answer
is: not in the slightest. Someone could declare Parliament to be in session in
the sovereign's name and the two houses would go about their business of
debate and legislation in exactly the same way. The speech would be deliv-
ered by the Lord Chancellor – much more appropriate since it is written by
the government and not by the Palace – the 'Humble Address' would be
moved and seconded, and the new parliamentary year would start in earnest
next day with the debate on the speech.

So why do we bother? Different people will give different answers, but they fall broadly into three groups: the traditionalists, the functionalists and the pragmatists. To express their views in the simplest form, the traditionalists believe that it is justified by precedent and antiquity. We have been doing it for hundreds of years and there is no reason to stop doing it now. It is a link with our past, a reminder of our history, and a celebration of the antiquity of our nation.

The functionalists, on the other hand, think it is a complete waste of time and ought to be abolished. It disrupts traffic, wastes busy people's time, costs money and performs no useful function. Indeed, they say, it does the reverse: it stimulates and sanctifies a morbid preoccupation with the past, and is a classic expression of the attitude of mind that holds Britain back from claiming full membership of the modern world. They may also add that it reinforces all that is worst in our social system and class divisions.

The pragmatists are more relaxed. They simply want to know how much it costs and how much it earns. They would probably come to the conclusion that it is currently justifiable. The coaches, robes, jewels and troops are all there anyway. The traffic disruption is certainly an entry in the debit column, as is the valuable time of such people as the Woman of the Bedchamber, Gold Stick in Waiting and the Master of the Horse; but the value to the tourist industry must be a considerable credit and probably leaves the operation with a comfortable, if invisible, profit. However, if the balance were to change, the pragmatists would see no point in retaining the ceremony.

All these points of view are perfectly sensible. You cannot prove any of them wrong. But they all have one thing in common: they take it for granted that pageants and ceremonies are merely something left over from our past – that they are just an elaborate show and do not play any useful part in the life of the country today. Are they wrong? Again you cannot prove it either way. But the British monarchy has evolved around a different belief. We do not have to share that belief, but we have to understand it if we are to understand what the monarchy is trying to do.

The belief, to put it simply, is that there is more to the government of a country than the practical business of passing laws and carrying them out. In fact, that part of the sovereign's job is more or less automatic; the Queen never takes sides in any debate and cannot in practice refuse to sign Acts of Parliament or to approve Orders in Council (see pages 43-4). But the belief behind the monarchy is that people look to their leaders for something more than the practical business of running the country efficiently. We have feelings and emotions as well – not just our private and personal feelings, but feelings as a nation: collective emotions, emotional needs we know our fellow citizens share. We feel love and hate, pride and shame, hope and fear not just privately at home and work but also collectively, as part of the nation we belong to. The belief behind the British monarchy is that, as a nation, we look to our leaders to share and satisfy those emotional needs as well as the practical need to be properly governed, and that one of the jobs of the monarchy is to meet that collective national need.

There is a constant interplay between national emotion and practical politics. In the 1970 general election the Conservatives won a surprise victory over Labour. Many people, including the defeated Labour Prime Minister Harold Wilson, believe the reason Labour lost was that England had just lost their World Cup match against West Germany a few days before. Obviously there is no logic in blaming the government for a football result, but it can deeply affect how a nation feels about itself; and if a nation feels dejected and frustrated on polling day, it is not unreasonable to believe a lot of people might take it out on the ballot paper.

If the only job of government were to run the country efficiently, we probably would not need the monarchy at all. Business efficiency would not require a State Opening of Parliament or the Queen's signature on statutes, or members of the government to attend formal Privy Council meetings. The late Richard Crossman clearly resented the fact that he and three cabinet colleagues had to travel from London to Balmoral in Scotland and back just to stand for a few minutes while the Queen gave formal approval to a series of Orders in Council. A team of operational researchers and work study experts with flow charts, job sheets and stopwatches could sort that one out in no time.

But making and administering laws are not enough on their own. They also have to be obeyed. Why should any of us obey the law? If it were only because we were afraid of being caught and punished, and for no other reason, then it would take a police state to frighten us into obedience. In fact, we obey the law because we accept that laws have to be obeyed. They are the laws of our country and, while it would be an exaggeration to say that all of us obey all the laws all the time with enthusiasm, certainly most of us obey most of the laws most of the time without complaint, and we expect everyone else to do the same. If immigrants come to live here but say they do not see why they have to obey our laws, they arouse deep national resentment, and that resentment is one among many ways in which we express our sense of nationhood.

Our sense of nationhood is the root from which the British monarchy grows. We take it for granted that the government of the day represents that sense of nationhood politically just as the Olympic team represents it athletically, but not every nation is so lucky. In the fortieth year of the Queen's reign the world was full of peoples whose sense of nationhood was in conflict with the government they lived under – the Kurds in Iraq, the Palestinians in Israel, the Ukrainians in the Soviet Union, the Croatians in Yugoslavia, the Sikhs in India. All of them are political volcanoes, not always active, but always dangerous, and never extinct until the sense of nationhood is itself extinguished.

The job of the monarchy is to unite our sense of nationhood with the authority of government. The sovereign is both Head of State and Head of the Nation, which means that the two roles are linked in a single person and a single office; you can't have one without the other. If the sovereign commands the respect, affection and loyalty of the nation, then those irrational but powerful emotions are simultaneously focused on the state (though by no means necessarily on the government of the day) and make for a stable, lawful and peaceful country. But, if the sovereign loses touch with the nation, then the state itself is in danger and up for grabs, as Louis XVI of France discovered in 1789 and Tsar Nicholas II of Russia in 1917. Of course this does not mean that countries with presidents instead of kings and queens do not feel national emotion; France, Germany and the United States have as much national pride and sense of nationhood as Britain, Holland or Norway. But the belief behind the British monarchy is that a popular and successful monarch and Royal Family have an advantage: that they can harness national pride to the political state more powerfully and more enduringly than a republic and a president.

But what does that involve? How do you do it? How do you know if you have done it successfully?

The State Opening of Parliament is not a bad place to start. After Trooping the Colour, it is the largest annual royal parade and it marks the beginning of the parliamentary year. But, as we have seen, it has nothing to do with the efficient functioning of government – so what is it for?

The first and simplest answer is that every tribe needs tribal events. It may not be logical, but it is universal. Towns and villages, churches and regiments, schools and colleges, offices and factories – all of them feel a need to create tribal occasions. They may be called parades, outings, dances, parties, galas, displays, carnivals, festivals or any other of a hundred names, but what they have in common is that they bring the whole tribe together for an event that is out of the everyday run of things. The State Opening is just such a tribal event: far larger, far more splendid, but still serving the basic tribal needs to let everyone see the whole tribe together, to create a joint experience and a shared memory, to affirm tribal membership and celebrate tribal unity and tribal values.

But every parade does something more than that. It makes a statement about the tribe. The old Soviet May Day parade of tanks, rockets, artillery and infantry made a clear statement: 'We have enormous military power and an aggressive military attitude.' When East–West relations thawed out, the militarism was rapidly toned down. In the same way, the State Opening of Parliament makes a statement, in fact a number of statements.

To start with, it makes a statement by what it celebrates: not the victory over a colonial power like the Americans on the Fourth of July or the overthrow of an oppressive and unpopular dynasty like the French on Bastille Day, but the orderly process of government starting its new year. It displays the king or queen to the people, which may sound a little unnecessary, but not many years ago the Chinese government felt it had to display an ageing Mao Tse-Tung just to prove he was still alive. But of course the main ceremony of the Opening of Parliament, once the procession has arrived at the Palace of Westminster, was not intended for the general public and was never seen by most of us until television cameras were allowed into the Houses of Parliament in 1958. It is a private ritual for the government tribe, the 1,000 or so most senior people at the centre of public affairs, and for them it is rich in symbolic actions and objects.

It symbolizes the supremacy of the sovereign: the Queen enters only when everyone else is present. They rise as she enters and do not sit until she is seated on the throne which is raised above the floor-level of the House.

It symbolizes the antiquity of the monarchy. In fact, the imperial state

BELOW The Yeomen of the Guard are the Queen's bodyguards.
Every year, since the Gunpowder Plot in 1605, they search the
vaults of Parliament. Nowadays they are joined by anti-terrorist
squads from the army and the police.
OVERLEAF The Queen is preceded to the throne by peers
holding the Cap of Maintenance (unseen) and the Sword of State.
The cap represents religious orthodoxy; the sword stands for her
intention to defend justice.

crown is made anew for every sovereign and they have the right to change the design, but some of the jewels are very ancient. It contains the Black Prince's ruby which Henry V wore at the Battle of Agincourt in 1415, a sapphire which reputedly belonged to Edward the Confessor nearly 1,000 years ago, the Stuart sapphire which James II took into exile and George IV bought back from a Venetian merchant, and three pearl drops which belonged to Elizabeth I.

It symbolizes continuity: not just by the crown jewels worn by sovereigns over so many centuries, but also through the form of the ceremony itself. The Queen puts the crown on in the Robing Room just before entering the House of Lords. For twenty-four years it was brought to her on a cushion by the sixth Marquess of Cholmondeley as Lord Great Chamberlain of England, but he died in 1989, so in 1990 it was brought in for the first time by the thirty-year-old seventh Marquess, who succeeded to the title and the office on his father's death. Some of the older members of the tribe will have attended the State Opening by the Queen's father and grandfather. An elderly peer might (just) have been a page when her great-grandfather Edward VII performed the ceremony, and today's pages, perhaps even the seventh Marquess of Cholmondeley (who will by then be ninety), may see it performed by her grandson in the second half of the next century.

It symbolizes lawful authority: civil authority – the sovereign as Head of State – through the Sword of State, and spiritual or religious authority – the sovereign as Head of the Church of England – through the Cap of Maintenance, each of which is held by a peer standing on either side of the throne. The cap is no problem, but the sword is so heavy it has to be supported by a sling; even so, it was too heavy for Field-Marshal Lord Montgomery of Alamein at the 1968 State Opening and a discreet substitute had to be brought on when he was seen to be swaying alarmingly.

It symbolizes the limited power of the sovereign: the shutting of the door of the Commons to Black Rod affirms the sovereign's constitutional acceptance that she has no right to enter their house. It demonstrates the

The Queen opens Parliament from her throne in the chamber of the House of Lords. It is the only true throne of the sovereign; the ones at Buckingham Palace and Windsor Castle are unofficial.

supremacy of Parliament and the independence of MPs and recalls Charles I's attempt to enter the Commons and arrest five Opposition members in 1642. The presence of both parties side by side in the Lords for the speech reflects the unity of the state, of which the Queen is the acknowledged and non-partisan head despite the political divisions within it. This is slightly confused for the ordinary television viewer by the fact that the Queen's speech sounds disturbingly like a party political broadcast for the government of the day.

All this is, of course, an attempt to express in plain language something that is being much more powerfully communicated by the unspoken rituals and symbols of the ceremony. Probably only a few of the spectators and viewers interpret the signals, but they get the message.

The ceremony and the order of procession are almost identical every year. This is part of the symbolic continuity: the individual people come and go – lords, ministers, sovereigns – but the framework of government remains unchanged. Indeed some of the offices, like Lord Great Chamberlain and Earl Marshal, pass from father to son. But there is also a practical reason: it would be almost impossible to create a completely new ceremony every year and have everyone learn and rehearse new parts. It would be risking disaster at every step. What makes it possible is that so many people have done it all before, some of them many times. Most ritual is, in fact, a sort of high-class routine. It is a bit like a travelling circus. When it arrives in each new town people do not have to work out new ways of setting up rings and marquees and stalls. It all goes up quickly and smoothly because everyone knows exactly what has to happen and what they have to do and when. It is another example of living ritual.

And is it worth all the time, trouble and rehearsal? That depends on whether you believe symbols and rituals have a place in our lives today. If you do not, the spectacle of so many sober senior citizens putting on fancy dress to take part in a pointless and protracted charade must look quite exceptionally absurd. Perhaps it does even to some of the participants. But if enough of them felt uncomfortable, it would be perfectly easy to stop it or update it as the Soviet Union recently updated its May Day parade. The fact that they do not change it suggests that a belief in the importance of symbol, ceremony and ritual is still firmly held by the elders of the ruling tribe.

A few days before the State Opening of Parliament the crown jewels
are collected from the Tower of London. They are checked and
polished before joining the procession to Parliament.
OVERLEAF Away from her formal role as Head of the State, the
Queen talks to children in Bracknell in her informal role as Head
of the Nation.

But whether you believe in it all or not, most people would agree that, if
it is going to be done, it might as well be done properly. You do not want
mangy horses, muddy boots, helmets falling off, and the whole parade
running two hours late and fetching up at the Tate Gallery instead of the
House of Lords. Walter Bagehot, writing about the English constitution in
1867, said: 'There are arguments for not having a Court, and there are
arguments for having a splendid Court, but there are no arguments for
having a mean Court. It is better to spend a million in dazzling when you
wish to dazzle, than three-quarters of a million in trying to dazzle and yet
not dazzling.' Or as a former Lord Chamberlain, Lord Cobbold, expressed
it: 'All ceremonial is ridiculous unless it is perfect.'

2

THE QUEEN
AND HER MINISTERS

On 27 November 1990, in one of the most sudden and surprising political upheavals of the Queen's forty-year reign, the parliamentary Conservative Party removed Margaret Thatcher from the premiership and replaced her with John Major.

Constitutionally, however, that is not what happened at all. A political party can elect a leader, but it cannot appoint a prime minister. John Major was only elected leader of his party. Margaret Thatcher remained Prime Minister even after she had withdrawn from the leadership contest on 22 November. She was still the Prime Minister five days later, after John Major had been declared Conservative Party leader. She only ceased to hold the office at 9.45 a.m. on 28 November, when she went to Buckingham Palace to offer her resignation to the Queen. In fact, it was her second visit; she had been there after the first leadership ballot to tell the Queen of her intention to resign. For forty-five minutes the country was

ABOVE The Queen talks to Douglas Hurd, Foreign and Commonwealth Secretary, before the 'G7' Summit Dinner at Buckingham Palace. The Palace does more business with the Foreign Office than with any other government department, including No 10 Downing Street.

Past and present: Prime Minister John Major talks to his predecessor,
Margaret Thatcher, and Sir Denis over pre-dinner drinks at
Buckingham Palace.

without a prime minister, until John Major arrived at 10.30 a.m., was shown
into the Audience Room, and accepted the Queen's invitation to form a
government.

And yet, in spite of all the constitutional niceties and proprieties, the truth
is that the Queen had no choice. Like most of her constitutional duties as
Head of State, her invitation to John Major was a formality. He was the
leader of a party with an absolute majority in the House of Commons and,
no matter whether she thought he was likely to be a brilliant leader or a
national disaster, she had to send for him. In the same way, although no Act
of Parliament can become law until she has signed it, she cannot in practice
refuse to; as Bagehot put it, writing of Queen Victoria, 'She must sign her
own death warrant if the two Houses put it up to her.'

But although the act of sending for John Major was a formality, it expressed
a distinction that is a reality – the distinction between state and government.
They do not have to be separate, but if they are fused into a single office and
function, both exercised by the same person or group, then any attempt to
overthrow the government of the day threatens the stability of the state.

Whatever else it may choose to do, every government has two inescapable duties: to preserve order within the realm and to defend its frontiers against attack. If it fails to do either, it soon stops being a government. Clearly, if state and government are the same thing, then the chances of internal dissent expressing itself as rebellion are significantly increased; but, if the actions (and members) of the government are visibly separate and distanced from those of the state, then the government can be challenged and, if necessary, removed while the ship of state sails serenely on. So parliamentary government is at root a device for preserving order within the realm: it institutionalizes party conflict and any individual leader or government is removable, while the monarchy institutionalizes national unity and is permanent. A general election resulting in a change of government is a sort of controlled revolution; it has been described as the only known method of changing governments without bloodshed. Every member of the government is removed virtually overnight. But the whole apparatus of the state continues unchanged: Her Majesty's civil service occupies the same offices and drives the same cars; they just have different government ministers in them. Her Majesty's judges continue to preside over the courts. The soldiers of the Queen continue to defend the realm, and convicted criminals continue to be detained in Her Majesty's prisons during Her Majesty's pleasure.

It follows that, if internal order is to continue to be preserved in this way, one of the central duties of the monarch is to preserve the distinction between the state and the government. This means that governments will always be controversial, challenging and confrontational, while the job of monarchy is to be uncontroversial, acceptable and agreeable. In particular it means being very careful about staying outside any political party conflict. Traditionally members of the Royal Family never vote. The Queen does not have a vote, but the others do – or rather they may have one if not otherwise disqualified. The relevant disqualification is membership of the House of Lords, which means that the Duke of Edinburgh, the Prince of Wales (as Duke of Cornwall) and the Duke of York are not entitled to vote, but Princess Anne and Prince

The Princess of Wales with Norma Major in Buckingham Palace. The monarchy provides the focus for the social life of the government community.

Edward are. In practice, of course, they never do; they all take extreme care to avoid any hint of party bias. The frontier line between state and government may be narrow, but, like the frontier between government and political party, it is heavily patrolled and jealously defended. Ministers of the Crown may not use government cars on party business (unless they are prominent enough to be terrorist targets) or use their civil servants to help them on party matters, and any suggestion that judges, top civil servants or other state officials are being appointed or promoted because they support the government party is met with howls of outrage.

The distinction between state and government is easier to define and preserve in a hereditary monarchy than in an elective presidency. Presidents like George Bush and François Mitterrand are identified with a single political party. They will have spent most of their careers in conflict and dispute. They will have made enemies. Millions of their fellow citizens will have consistently voted against them. It is hard to represent the unity of a nation with such a history of faction and controversy. And, if there is a political

Kenneth Baker, Home Secretary, at a 'dine and sleep' visit to Windsor Castle in April 1991. Guests are invited to browse in the library after dinner.

scandal like Watergate, then it is not just the government that is threatened – the whole state is in turmoil. In Britain it is one thing to question the honesty of the prime minister and quite another to question the integrity of the sovereign. In the United States they are in effect the same person. Watergate paralysed the whole apparatus of state. A similar political scandal would have convulsed the *government* of Britain, but the state, for example in the conduct of foreign affairs, would not have been crippled in the same way.

So, if the Queen is to preserve this important distinction between state and government, she has to be free of even the faintest suspicion of party favouritism. She has no vote, but could not use it if she had. Her Private Secretaries have to study every invitation to visit an organization or to patronize a charity in order to make absolutely sure that acceptance could not be seen as supporting any political party. This applies to every member of the family. The report of an alleged private, off-the-cuff comment by the Prince of Wales in favour of proportional representation – the policy of the Social and Liberal Democratic Party – created a press outcry and raised the temperature of the body politic several degrees.

Neither the distinction between state and nation nor the division of roles between sovereign and prime minister is natural or obvious. Both have taken centuries to evolve into their present form. It is a sophisticated distinction. An absolute monarchy or a military dictatorship is much easier to understand; it is the way most nations begin their existence. But in Britain over the centuries the absolute power of the sovereign has been steadily whittled away. In 1215 the Magna Carta set down the limits of the King's rights under the law; in 1265 Simon de Montfort made the King listen to the views of his people by summoning the knights from the shires to Parliament; the victory of the Parliamentarians in the Civil War meant that after the restoration of Charles II in 1660 no king could raise taxes unless Parliament voted for them; and the expulsion of the Catholic James II in 1688 in favour of the Protestant William and Mary was final proof that the will of the nation outweighed the

OVERLEAF Following a dinner for distinguished guests, the Queen in conversation in Windsor Castle library. Her constitutional right to be consulted, to encourage and to warn makes her experience available to every government.

The Queen talks to Neil Kinnock, Labour Party leader, after dinner
in the library at Windsor. Although the government is Her Majesty's
Government, the opposition is also Her Majesty's Opposition. The
Queen keeps strict political neutrality.

The Prime Minister meets another predecessor: John Major and
Edward Heath at a Buckingham Palace dinner for the members of
the 'G7' economic summit in July 1991.

power of the sovereign. Forty-six years of two often absentee German kings – George I (1714–27) and George II (1727–60) – emphasized the distinction and dramatically shifted the balance of political power from the sovereign to the government of the day. In many cases the powers have not been formally removed; the Queen could, in theory, disband the army, sell all the ships in the navy, dismiss the civil service, give the Channel Islands to France, pardon every prisoner and make everyone a peer. In practice, however, she can do none of these things without the formal advice of her government, which she would be unlikely to receive. In spite of this, there still remain two powers which the sovereign may have to use independently – that is to say without, or even conceivably against, the advice of her prime minister. They are rare, but they are real and, because they bring the sovereign very close to direct political intervention, they are highly sensitive.

The first is the power to send for a member of the House of Commons (or, in theory, the House of Lords) and ask him or her to form a government. In John Major's case there was no problem – he was the elected leader of the party which held an absolute majority in the House of Commons. But twice in her forty-year reign it was not so clear-cut. In 1963, when Harold Macmillan resigned as Prime Minister because of illness, the parliamentary Conservative Party had no agreed method for electing a leader to take over the premiership. There was no obvious successor, although it was generally assumed that Rab Butler was his number two. The problem was that, once Macmillan had stated his intention to resign, he could not give formal 'Advice' to the Queen, the sort she must constitutionally accept. He could, however, give 'advice' with a small 'a' – informal guidance – which he did. He took soundings (largely through intermediaries, since he was in bed in hospital) and drew up a memorandum. He then resigned formally and, *after* resigning, read the memorandum to the Queen in his hospital ward. His advice (but not his Advice) was that Alec Douglas-Home was the right choice. Technically the Queen was not bound by this advice, but in practice she had little choice but to accept it. The question then was whether Douglas-Home could form a government, which in practice meant whether he could persuade Rab Butler to serve under him. So the Queen sent for Douglas-Home and asked him if he could. Butler decided not to risk splitting the government and the Conservative Party, so he agreed, and Douglas-Home became Prime Minister. Some of Butler's senior supporters – Iain MacLeod

From left to right: Kenneth Baker, Glenys and Neil Kinnock and
Rear-Admiral Sir Paul Greening, Master of the Queen's Household.
The Conservative Party and the Labour Party associate
amicably after the royal dinner party.

in particular – expressed their outrage in public and, although it was against
the party and not the sovereign, there was still a feeling that the Queen had
come dangerously close to the frontier even though it was the system which
compelled her to do so.

Eleven years later there was a potentially even more dangerous predica-
ment. At least the conflict in 1963 was entirely within the Conservative
Party. In 1974 the general election gave neither party a working majority.
In the event there was no crisis. Tory leader Edward Heath with 297 seats
tried to come to an agreement with the minority parties, but failed. Labour

leader Harold Wilson with 301 seats then faced the House of Commons and defeated a motion of no confidence. If they had both failed, the Queen would no doubt have granted a dissolution of Parliament. But, if another general election, or two more, produced the same result, the Queen would have been in great difficulty. Perhaps a senior politician in one of the major parties could have formed a government, possibly a coalition. The only final test is whether someone can survive a vote of no confidence in the House. But first of all the Queen has to send for them and ask them to try, and even if she is acting on advice, she is not acting on government 'Advice' and comes perilously close to direct political action.

And suppose Margaret Thatcher had decided to stay on as Prime Minister after being replaced as leader of her party? She has said that the thought did indeed cross her mind. Constitutionally she was entitled to do so, and if she had asked for a vote of confidence and, with the help of her Conservative supporters and mischievous Opposition MPs, received such a vote – highly unlikely, but not theoretically impossible – what would happen then? Could the elected leader of the majority party be denied the premiership? The Queen could hardly dismiss a prime minister who had received a vote of confidence from the House, and several prime ministers have not been leaders of the majority party in the Commons: Lloyd George from 1916 to 1922, Ramsay MacDonald from 1931 to 1935, and Winston Churchill in 1940. Mrs Thatcher would have been able to continue, but the outrage of the Conservative MPs who had voted against her would have been wonderful to behold.

A *British* prime minister with a majority in the lower house has never been dismissed since William IV effectively dismissed Melbourne in 1834; and yet the Crown has dismissed a prime minister with just such a majority. It was not the Queen's personal decision, but it was taken under her constitutional authority as Queen of Australia in 1975 by the Governor General when he dismissed Gough Whitlam, the Australian Prime Minister, after he had failed to get his budget through the (elected) senate and it looked as if the

OVERLEAF The Queen and the Duke of Edinburgh open the New Zealand Parliament. The Queen's ministers are not confined to Britain; she is Queen of seventeen of the fifty Commonwealth countries.

government would be unable to pay its bills. The Governor General was able to do this without reference to the Queen because he is more like a viceroy than an ambassador. He possesses most of the powers of the Crown. The wounds this dismissal created are still raw, but, because he was following Australia's written constitution, there was no choice.

There is, however, the Queen's second remaining power of intervention in day-to-day politics: the power to dissolve Parliament. Parliament is dissolved at the request, not on the 'Advice', of the Prime Minister. It is normally automatic and granted whenever the Prime Minister asks for it. But suppose there had already been two recent general elections resulting in no party winning a clear majority, and suppose a Prime Minister were to ask for a third election out of pig-headedness or self-preservation when it was not necessary or in the interests of the country? In such a case the Queen would be within her constitutional rights to refuse a dissolution of Parliament and tell him to get on with it, and if 'getting on with it' resulted in a defeat in the House of Commons, then she could invite someone else to try to survive a motion of no confidence and avoid a third general election.

It is even possible that the Queen could insist on a dissolution of Parliament against the wish of the government. If, for example, a government proposed a major constitutional change – abolition of the House of Lords, say, or even of the monarchy – which was not in its pre-election manifesto and for which it had no popular mandate, then if it was clearly unpopular in the country the Queen would probably be entitled to insist on a general election before such a fundamental change were carried out. But since it has never happened, we do not know.

The five days from 12 to 16 June 1987 were quite an eventful period in the career of Rhodes Boyson. He began it as Dr Rhodes Boyson MP, a member of the government, and ended it as the Right Honourable Dr Sir Rhodes Boyson PC, MP, a backbencher. He had lost his job, been given a knighthood in recognition of past services – fairly normal for retiring or sacked junior ministers – and been made a member of Her Majesty's Privy Council, which is automatic for members of the cabinet, but a special honour for non-cabinet ministers.

What exactly is the point of the Privy Council? Its origins can be traced

Within five days in 1987 Dr Rhodes Boyson MP, a government
minister, turned into the Rt Hon. Dr Sir Rhodes Boyson PC, MP, a
backbencher. Here he holds his badge of knighthood after his
investiture, having been 'sworn of the Privy Council' the previous day.

back over 1,000 years, to Alfred the Great, who came to the throne in AD
871. Once it was the most powerful body in the land, the gathering of the
sovereign's most influential and trusted advisers, but over the years its powers
have been steadily removed. Today its duties are mere formalities and
membership is an honour rather than a responsibility; it has been described
as the most prestigious rubber stamp in the kingdom. It is, though, one of
the Queen's constitutional duties to head it. Is it a complete waste of time?

Its main job is to make Orders in Council. Acts of Parliament often give
the government powers to make further regulations by Order in Council

rather than by going back to Parliament and laboriously passing new laws. This means that about once a month four counsellors – usually but not necessarily cabinet ministers – are summoned by the Clerk to the Privy Council to attend on the Queen wherever she happens to be. They stand throughout the whole proceeding, which is usually only about ten minutes. (This useful device for keeping meetings short was instituted by Queen Victoria after Prince Albert died in 1861.) The Lord President of the Council reads out each order, the Queen calls out 'Approved' and a new proposal becomes law. The only exception to this is the appointment of High Sheriffs. They are 'pricked': their names are listed on a twenty-foot roll of starched cartridge paper and the Queen pierces it against the name of each county sheriff designate with a bodkin. The practice is supposed to date back to an occasion when Elizabeth I was asked to approve the appointment of sheriffs while she was sewing, and her bodkin was the only available marking instrument. (Not many needleworkers would recognize the implement the Queen actually wields: it is a three-inch steel spike set in a sort of brass doorknob and weighs nearly twelve ounces.)

All very colourful, and no doubt necessary to give legal force to government decisions and regulations, but could it not all be done at a desk with a signature in front of a witness? In practical terms, yes, it almost certainly could, but there is a case for the formality and solemnity. To start with, some momentous decisions are taken by Order in Council without needing the approval of Parliament: for instance, making treaties, mobilizing the armed forces, declaring a state of emergency and declaring war. Most people would be happier to know that such decisions were taken by a meeting of senior statesmen in the presence of the Queen than just by pieces of paper sent over to the Palace from Downing Street. Even for less important decisions people are likely to think much harder about drafting orders carefully if they are to be read out to the Queen in Council. It also provides a convenient oppor-tunity for the Queen to meet and talk to members of the government other than the Prime Minister.

There is, however, another less formal side to the Privy Council, and that is the fact of membership. This too is ritualized. Rhodes Boyson did not simply open an envelope, read the good news, and go off and get his stationery reprinted; he had to be 'sworn of the Privy Council'. This meant attending one of its meetings, and swearing the Oath of Allegiance. It is taken kneeling on a footstool. He then gets up and moves to another footstool just in front of the Queen, where he kneels again and kisses hands (actually just brushing the back of her hand with his lips). After that he returns to his original standing position and takes the Oath of the Privy Counsellor. This oath is secret, but it is known to be the longest oath in existence. When it finally comes to an end, he shakes hands with his colleagues and is a fully fledged and sworn-in Privy Counsellor. Again, membership could be conferred like membership of American Express simply by sending a card and declaration form through the post. The purpose of the ceremony, therefore, is to emphasize the importance of membership by solemn ceremony. But is it important? Perhaps it is not as important as all of its members would like to think, but there is at least one purpose it serves which is probably very useful and the more so for not being widely publicized.

The British political system is rooted in division and confrontation. The electoral system is meant to give the best chance of a clear majority to a single party. There is a government and an opposition facing each other across the House, not a lot of different parties ranged in a semicircle in front of a podium. To most of the public, politics looks like a constant, bitter war, and yet obviously there are occasions when members of the government have to talk to their counterparts on the opposition front bench. They may have to give them secret information in confidence. How do they know if they can trust them? That assurance is given by the Privy Council oath. They talk to each other 'on a Privy Counsellor basis'. Council membership is a device for achieving agreement and unity between the opposing parties in private, while in public they carry on the party battle unabated. Nobody pretends it heals the divisions, but it provides a useful bridge across them. It is certainly one of the ways in which a strictly non-partisan monarchy can influence the conduct of government without direct legislative action. The Privy Council has nearly 400 members, mostly senior British and Commonwealth statesmen, and provides a foundation of common purpose and shared membership on which we have built the structured adversary politics of Her Majesty's Government and Her Majesty's Opposition.

3

THE CONFIDENTIAL CONSULTANT

On Wednesday 5 December 1990 John Major was driven from 10 Downing Street to Buckingham Palace. He arrived at the King's Door, on the right-hand side of the courtyard, at 6.30 p.m. and was met by the Queen's Private Secretary. They went up to the Empire Room. An equerry came to say that the Queen was ready to receive her ninth Prime Minister, and he was shown into the Audience Room, where the Queen was waiting. The meeting lasted about an hour and a quarter, after which he was taken down to the Private Secretary's office, where the two Private Secretaries, his own and the Queen's, were waiting. They chatted for a few minutes over a drink and then Major was driven back to Downing Street.

It may seem unusual for either the Queen or the Prime Minister to have meetings in their official capacity at which no assistant, secretary or other official is present, but no third party ever attends the Prime Minister's regular

ABOVE Prime Minister John Major had just returned from trips to Moscow and then Beijing, where he had been discussing the future of Hong Kong with the Chinese government, when he went for his regular audience with the Queen at Balmoral Castle in September 1991.

An eighty-year-old Prime Minister says goodbye to his twenty-seven-
year-old Queen after dinner at 10 Downing Street. The Queen had
been on the throne for three years; Winston Churchill had
entered Parliament fifty-five years earlier, when her father
George VI was a five-year-old.

Tuesday audience with the Queen (this one was held on a Wednesday because of the exceptional circumstances). If either of them keeps any written notes of what passes between them, no one else knows about it; nothing is preserved in the official records. What do they talk about? For all that anyone else in the world knows, the whole hour may be passed in the genial exchange of empty pleasantries. Certainly it does not involve any formal duties – nothing has to be submitted, approved, signed or authorized, and it fulfils no formal role in the process of government. It may, for all anyone except the Queen, John Major and the other five living ex-prime ministers knows, be a purely social encounter.

But is that likely? Can we really believe that two people at the head of the affairs of a nation of some fifty-seven million people will find nothing to talk about week after week and year after year except the state of the weather and the health of their children? And if they do discuss matters of substance and significance, exactly what is the role of the sovereign at that meeting?

One thing we can be quite sure about is that the Queen's contribution to that meeting will have changed very considerably over the forty years of her reign. She gave her first audience to Winston Churchill in 1952, when she was twenty-five years old. She was not exactly a novice, but neither was she born to the job; until Edward VIII's abdication crisis blew up, it had seemed most improbable that she would ever succeed to the throne. By contrast her first Prime Minister had been a member of the government forty-seven years before her accession and had been Chancellor of the Exchequer before she was born. He had, in fact, taken part in the last cavalry charge of the British Army at the battle of Omdurman in 1898. If there was any element of teacher and pupil in the relationsip, it is quite clear who was which.

It was very different in 1990. John Major was nine years old when the Queen gave her first audience to Winston Churchill. Major's first Prime Minister's audience was getting on for her 1,200th in forty years of weekly private meetings with Churchill, Anthony Eden, Harold Macmillan, Alec Douglas-Home, Harold Wilson, Edward Heath, James Callaghan and Margaret Thatcher. Forty years of reading government papers and Foreign Office telegrams. Forty years of conversations with emperors, kings, presidents, prime ministers, ambassadors and high commissioners. John Major had only been a cabinet minister for three years and for all but three months of that time he had been in the Treasury. In fact, no living British politician can begin to match the Queen's knowledge of state secrets because politicians have access to them only when they are in office (unless they are shown them by the government 'on a Privy Counsellor basis'), and even then they are not allowed access to papers of the other party's administration. The Queen is never out of office.

It is of course perfectly possible that the weekly audience is purely a briefing session in which the Prime Minister gives the Queen the confidential background information on the events of the week and the papers she has received, and that the Queen is simply a passive recipient with no input of her own. Certainly she does not have the power to initiate or prohibit any government legislation, but, when almost all other powers had been stripped from the monarchy and handed over to the two Houses of Parliament, the sovereign retained three constitutional rights: the right to be consulted, the right to encourage, and the right to warn. No specific place or time is provided by the constitution for the exercise of these three rights, but you do not have to look very far to find the easiest and most obvious time and place: 6.30 p.m. on Tuesday in the Audience Room at Buckingham Palace.

The Queen, as we know, takes no active part in the day-to-day process of government, but that does not mean there is no value for the Prime Minister in having a regular meeting with her. If nothing else, it ensures that once a week he takes a few minutes out of the frantic urgency of day-to-day politics to reflect on the past week, and to identify, analyse and talk about the key issues, events and decisions. For Winston Churchill in 1952 that may have been the principal and almost the only value of the audience, but for John Major in 1990 it is likely to have been something more.

The Queen is not normally thought of as a political consultant, but from a prime minister's point of view she is a unique confidante. She is clearly enormously well informed, completely trustworthy and secure, and as deeply involved in and committed to the good of the country as he is. She travels regularly all round the United Kingdom, visiting its institutions, talking to assorted luminaries and dignitaries as well as to ordinary men and women in factories, hospitals, schools, charities and service units. She has visited over fifty foreign heads of state during her reign, and over sixty have visited her, not to mention hundreds, perhaps thousands, of ambassadors. In addition she has made over 100 Commonwealth visits. Not a bad cv for a government adviser. And on top of all that – and unlike almost all the other people with remotely comparable qualifications – she is not in any way competitive with the Prime Minister. She is not after his job.

It is hard to believe that any prime minister would not find it useful from time to time to talk things over with an adviser with these qualifications, to think out loud about forthcoming problems, to use the Queen as a sounding board. It is also hard to believe that she does not do something more than that. You do not have to be a brilliant political scientist to observe that the British political system is more heavily weighted in favour of short-term political expediency than long-term national good. A government's political horizon is never more than five years, and it gets shorter every day. A cabinet minister's political life hangs on a thread. On 21 November Margaret Thatcher had a majority of nearly 100 seats, she had won three general elections in a row, and she did not have to go to the country for another eighteen months. On 28 November she was just another backbench MP. In such an insecure occupation it is hardly surprising if short-term issues are in the front of the mind, at the head of the agenda and on the top of the first red dispatch box.

This is not to argue that prime ministers deliberately or thoughtlessly ignore long-term issues, only to recognize that the important usually has to take second place to the urgent. But the Queen does not have a short-term horizon; she will be on the throne until she literally draws her last breath. She has seen from the inside the effects of forty years of government decisions on the country in the long term. And every Tuesday she has the opportunity to talk to the Prime Minister and encourage him to think of long-term national benefits rather than, or at least as well as, short-term political survival. We do not know if she takes the opportunity, but, if she does, it is a constitutional way of balancing the short term against the long term. It is not, in fact, very different in principle from the relationship between the chairman and managing director of a corporation: the managing director is concerned with this year's results and next year's development plans, while the chairman is (or should be) thinking about the long-term financial health of the company and its identity, reputation, values and stability. They may have the same objectives, but they have a very different perspective and emphasis. The contrast between their two roles and responsibilities leads to one of the most important dialogues in the life of a corporation. There should also be a place for it in the life of a nation.

Margaret Thatcher at a Buckingham Palace reception in July 1991.
Mrs Thatcher was Prime Minister for more than a quarter of the
Queen's reign.
OVERLEAF In September 1991 the Prime Minister, John Major,
visited Balmoral for his regular audience with the Queen. He was
nine years old when the Queen held her first prime minister's
audience – with Winston Churchill. She has now held well over 1,000
audiences with nine prime ministers.

There are other questions the Queen might raise. She is after all the
Head of the judiciary, the armed forces, the Church of England and the
Commonwealth. They might have anxieties they want the Queen to com-
municate. This does not necessarily mean that they would want her to try
and argue the Prime Minister out of a declared course of action – or at least
no one would put it like that – but, if they were really unhappy about some
fundamental government reorganization of, say, the British Army or the
legal profession, they would not be stepping outside their spheres of responsibility in making their anxieties known to the Queen. We certainly know that
Field-Marshal Haig left George V in no doubt about his opinion of the
politicians during the First World War. The sovereign could suggest that
there might be facts which had not been drawn to the Prime Minister's

attention, arguments that had not been put to him, possible consequences of which his advisers had not warned him. Even very senior important people cannot always get the Prime Minister's ear; they cannot know if their papers are reaching him in the form in which they sent them, what comments may have been put on them, or what other and possibly mistaken or biased advice he is being given. If an issue seemed momentous to them, it is not ridiculous to guess that they might find the Palace a more dependable route than Whitehall to ensure that, if the government does take the wrong decision, it does not take it in ignorance. It is unlikely that they would get a decision changed in that way, but the time to affect a decision is before it is taken, while opinions are forming; and although most of us know nothing about such discussions until the decision has in effect been taken, the people at the head of the law, the Church and the armed forces will have been consulted and will therefore know that something is in the wind. Does it happen like that? We are all free to guess, but only the Queen, John Major and his five surviving predecessors actually know – and they are not telling.

On Tuesday 21 May 1991 the High Commissioner for Tanzania came to present his Letters of Commission to the Queen. Every ambassador has to do this (high commissioners are ambassadors from Commonwealth countries) before being entitled to represent his country officially in Britain or, to be technically accurate, at the Court of St James. It is not just a question of turning up one morning and seeing if the Queen happens to be in. Three state landaus are sent to his residence for him and his staff, and the Marshal of the Diplomatic Corps accompanies him to the Palace; he is

OPPOSITE ABOVE The Queen always spends the last part of each summer at Balmoral Castle in the Scottish Highlands. The castle was bought privately for the Royal Family by Prince Albert in 1852. BELOW 'After you, Ma'am.' The Queen shows her weekend guest round the flower garden at Balmoral during his first visit. OVERLEAF Every new ambassador to Britain has to visit Buckingham Palace and 'present his credentials' – his authority from his home government to represent it. This time it is the new US ambassador. He is in the White Drawing-Room, with the Permanent Under-Secretary of the Foreign and Commonwealth Office in attendance.

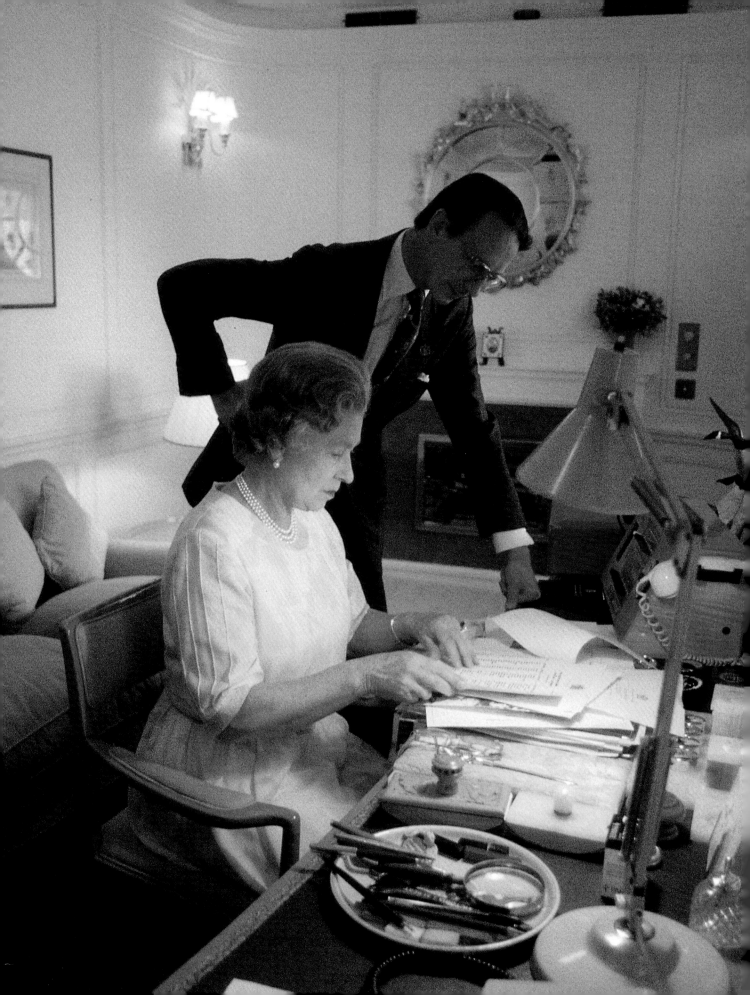

greeted by the Master of the Household, who takes him to the Bow Room, where he meets the Foreign Secretary or a top Foreign Office official. Flanked by the Marshal and the Master of the Household, he is conducted into the White Drawing Room, where the Queen is waiting. They take a pace forward. They bow. They take another pace forward. They bow again. He is then announced. He goes up to the Queen, bows a third time, shakes hands and presents his Letters of Commission and his predecessor's letters of recall. After that the atmosphere thaws out. They talk (in English or French) privately, he presents his staff, his wife is then introduced and presented, and after a few minutes' conversation they withdraw, turning at the door to bow once again before they leave.

Or at least that is what is supposed to happen. But, on Tuesday 21 May 1991, the Queen was in the USA, and since you evidently cannot have unaccredited ambassadors and high commissioners wandering about all over the place, the ceremony had to go ahead without her.

Obviously this was something which had happened before. The constitutional arrangement is that, in the sovereign's absence, two Counsellors of State act for her. They are members of the Royal Family, but their royal powers are severely limited: for example they can attend functions, carry out investitures, receive ambassadors and sign certain state papers, but they are not empowered to appoint a prime minister, dissolve Parliament, award honours or disband regiments. On this occasion the Prince of Wales and the Duke of York acted as Counsellors. In 1989, when the Queen was away at the Commonwealth Conference in Kuala Lumpur, it had been the Prince of Wales and the Queen Mother, one from a generation older than she and one from a generation younger. It symbolized the monarchy as a family business. It also raised the question of the hereditary principle. Is it right for a democracy to be presided over by someone who is never elected, does not

---

Official papers requiring the Queen's attention are sent to her every day, wherever she is. The Queen's Private Secretary, Sir Robert Fellowes, discusses them with her on HMY *Britannia* anchored off Miami, Florida, during the state visit to the USA in 1991.
OVERLEAF The Queen returns from a flying visit to Belfast. The plane becomes a temporary office while the Queen catches up on official business.

achieve the office by competitive examination or selection interview, and can never legally be removed or replaced?

A hereditary monarchy is not democratic or classless. It is not a job that is open to everyone or awarded to the best qualified. If those are the ultimate tests of the value of an institution then monarchy fails abysmally. But there are other standards, and to understand the role of the hereditary principle in the British monarchy it is important to examine them even if you do not accept them or consider them as valuable as the more democratic virtues.

If an office is not hereditary, it must be open to election in some form. A successor has to be appointed or chosen. This can leave a vacuum at the top when the old leader dies, and can provoke damaging competition. 'In an elective monarchy', wrote the historian Edward Gibbon in *The Decline and Fall of the Roman Empire*, 'the vacancy of the throne is a moment big with danger and mischief.' Gibbon was writing before 1789 (just), but the French experience of replacing a hereditary form of government with an elective

The Queen 'doing her boxes' in 1959. The Queen's official papers are sent up to her in a government red despatch box at the end of every working day. They come from Commonwealth countries as well as all the departments of the UK government.

The Queen 'doing her boxes' as she has for forty years, this time in
the Queen's Audience Room at Buckingham Palace. Some papers
she signs officially, some she writes comments on, some she
simply takes note of.

one by revolution did not contradict his pronouncement. And even in a
stable modern republic like the United States, the last year or two of a
president's second term, the 'lame duck' period, are well recognized as a
time of creeping governmental paralysis. A hereditary system avoids all these
problems. It does not merely provide a formula for deciding on a legal
successor, it also means that everybody knows well in advance who the
successor (barring accidents) is going to be. There is no argument about it.

It also means that the successor is likely to have been apprenticed to the job from birth. In fact, the present Queen did not become heir to the throne until she was ten years old, and her father had been heir for less than a year before his accession. Even so, they had always been shareholders in the family business as it were; they were always a focus of national interest though they only stepped late into the centre of the frame. The present Prince of Wales has been heir apparent from the day he was born and, if the fates are kind, we may expect Prince William to be king into the 2070s. The system provides stability because it is predictable. And even if the fates are unkind, the system makes certain there will be someone to pick up the sceptre. A family gives continuity and the power of renewal, even if it does not provide democracy and equality. It also makes political assassination a fairly futile activity, not just because the sovereign has so little direct political power but also because there are so many people to get rid of. There are some 200 living descendants of Queen Victoria in the established line of succession. They include Norwegians, Romanians, Yugoslavs, Russians, Swedes and Danes. Not all of her descendants are involved in conventional 'royal' occupations: at the latest official count in 1989, no 32 was a rock musician in New Mexico, no 35 was a record producer with Virgin Records, no 42 was a Montessori school teacher, no 51 was a teenage Norwegian schoolboy, and no 65 was a farm labourer in Sussex. But it is perfectly possible to go back well beyond that. It was calculated in 1911 that there were probably about 100,000 living descendants of Edward III, who died in 1377, and that number is hardly likely to have decreased. Who knows how many of us may not have some royal ancestry? The Queen's family tree can be traced back along the female line as far as a Frances Webb of Oaksey in Wiltshire, who married a Thomas Salisbury in 1795. It would, however, take an awful lot of assassinations to put one of those Wiltshire Webbs on the throne.

No matter how large the Royal Family may be, the number recognized as 'royals' by the nation at large is probably around thirty – people whose conduct would be seen as in some way reflecting on the monarchy. It is a small proportion of the traceable heirs, but it is still quite a substantial number of people; certainly large enough to form an institution on its own. It is in a way a strange family to belong to, and even stranger perhaps to marry into. They are intimately involved, day after day, with powerful people, dignified institutions and important issues at the heart of Britain's affairs and yet forbidden to take any part in political debate. They are chained to the uncontroversial. It can make for bland platitudes in public speeches, but, as we have already seen, the fact of being excluded from party politics, together with the knowledge that they will be royals all their lives, helps them to focus on the long term rather than the short term, the permanent rather than the transitory. They find opportunities in subjects like architecture, the environment, inner cities, the underprivileged young, health and educational charities, where they believe they can see problems building up in the years to come, but which have not yet become party issues in the political arena.

It was said of General de Gaulle that he loved France, but did not much like the French. This is a useful distinction. When we talk about 'the will of the British people', we are usually only talking about it at this particular moment. For politicians it is the only practical view to take. But there is also the will of the British people in twenty or fifty years' time – the ones who will not, for example, be able to will back vanished forests and dried-up lakes. De Gaulle sometimes saw the contemporary French political scene as a squalid and ignoble interlude between his beloved country's great history and its great destiny. It is not a democratic or politically popular way of looking at one's country, but it is a useful counterweight to the tyranny of the mood of the moment and the snap judgement. As Francis Bacon, the Elizabethan writer, once observed, 'Counsels to which Time hath not been called, Time will not ratify.' Only a fine line separates the popular democrat from the unprincipled vote-seeker, and there is always a danger that long-term benefit will be sacrificed to short-term popularity. A hereditary system and a royal family mean that there is at least one sizeable group of people in an influential position whose job compels them to look at the country from a vantage point that is not easily achieved by those who are caught up in the frantic bustle of day-to-day political life.

4

FOREIGN
EXCHANGES

At 8.30 p.m. on Tuesday 23 April 1991 the Queen and a former shipyard electrician from Gdansk in northern Poland sat down together to dinner in St George's Hall, Windsor Castle. They were not alone: there were 150 guests and 300 staff on duty to serve them. The state banquet for the state visit of the President of the Republic of Poland and Mrs Walesa was under way.

British state banquets are not the world's largest or most lavish, but for the western world at least they are still the model of how it should be done: when in doubt, find out how they do it at Buckingham Palace – which is in fact a much more frequent venue than Windsor for such banquets. As with most ceremonial events, the pattern remains almost unchanged over the years and indeed the generations. Innovation is sacrificed to efficiency – unless it increases smoothness, like the traffic lights. These are amber and green lights concealed inside the large flower arrangements in two corners of the 123-foot-long Ballroom at Buckingham Palace, where state banquets are

ABOVE Commonwealth Day, 11 March 1991. The Queen attends an evening reception at Lancaster House. The Commonwealth has representatives from all the world's main regions except the Middle East.

The King's Troop of the Royal Horse Artillery wait for the Polish
President's procession to arrive at Windsor Castle.
OVERLEAF Lech Walesa, President of Poland, drives up the Royal
Mile at Windsor at the start of his state visit in April 1991.
Arrangements for the three-day visit filled a 103-page booklet which
was issued to everyone involved.

held. Amber is the signal from the Palace Steward, who stands immediately
behind the Queen, for the seventy-six servers to take their positions – four
at each of the nineteen 'service stations'. Green is the signal for them to start
serving or clearing.

Planning a state banquet begins several months in advance, but this tends
to be the diplomatic activity – determining who to invite, which entails the
thankless job of deciding who will be left out. It also means finding out about
special menus. The Palace chefs are experts on the different dietary laws of
the world's religions, but someone has to tell them if any guest happens to
be a vegan, a diabetic, or has a peptic ulcer or gout. All these details and
hundreds of others are sorted out on a 'proving trip', a reconnaissance visit
by officials from the visiting country armed with long lists of questions,
matched by equally long lists prepared by the host country.

It is more than a little bit like a theatrical production: the casting and
costing take place well in advance, but the real activity rises to a climax in

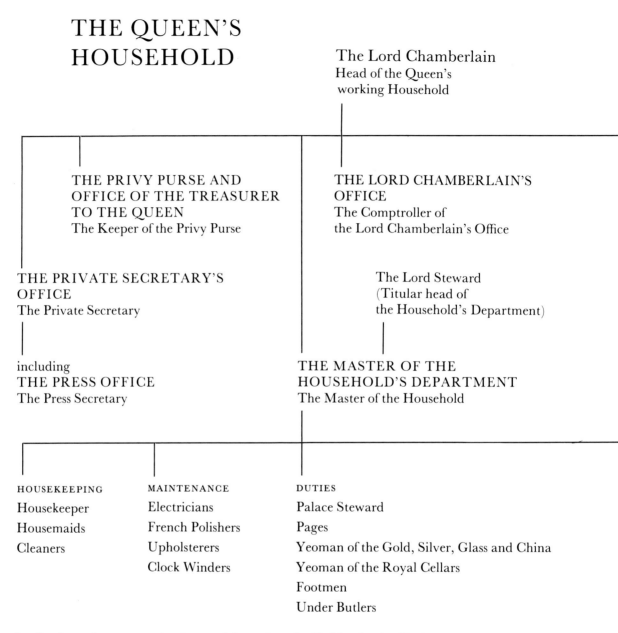

THE QUEEN'S HOUSEHOLD

The Lord Chamberlain
Head of the Queen's
working Household

**THE PRIVY PURSE AND
OFFICE OF THE TREASURER
TO THE QUEEN**
The Keeper of the Privy Purse

**THE LORD CHAMBERLAIN'S
OFFICE**
The Comptroller of
the Lord Chamberlain's Office

**THE PRIVATE SECRETARY'S
OFFICE**
The Private Secretary

The Lord Steward
(Titular head of
the Household's Department)

including
THE PRESS OFFICE
The Press Secretary

**THE MASTER OF THE
HOUSEHOLD'S DEPARTMENT**
The Master of the Household

HOUSEKEEPING	MAINTENANCE	DUTIES
Housekeeper	Electricians	Palace Steward
Housemaids	French Polishers	Pages
Cleaners	Upholsterers	Yeoman of the Gold, Silver, Glass and China
	Clock Winders	Yeoman of the Royal Cellars
		Footmen
		Under Butlers

the final week or two. And, as with a play, it divides logically into two parts: what the public – the guests – are supposed to see, and what goes on behind the scenes. The stage – the Ballroom at Buckingham Palace or St George's Hall at Windsor Castle – is the province of the Master of the Household, working (like everyone else) under the Lord Chamberlain. The Lord Chamberlain is a sort of non-executive chairman of the monarchy. In political and constitutional matters and in much of her day-to-day business the

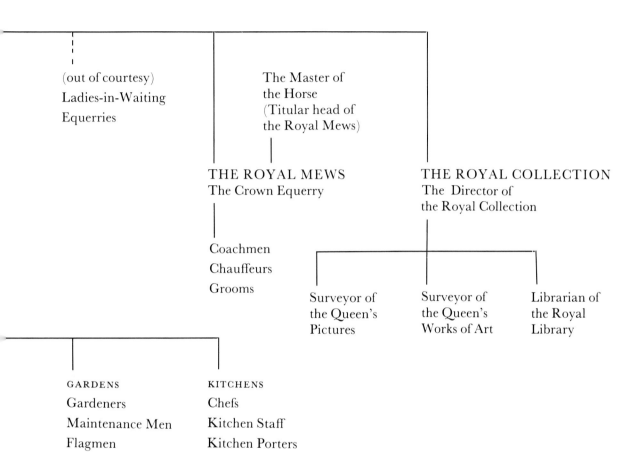

(out of courtesy)
Ladies-in-Waiting
Equerries

The Master of
the Horse
(Titular head of
the Royal Mews)

THE ROYAL MEWS
The Crown Equerry

THE ROYAL COLLECTION
The Director of
the Royal Collection

Coachmen
Chauffeurs
Grooms

Surveyor of
the Queen's
Pictures

Surveyor of
the Queen's
Works of Art

Librarian of
the Royal
Library

GARDENS
Gardeners
Maintenance Men
Flagmen

KITCHENS
Chefs
Kitchen Staff
Kitchen Porters

Queen deals directly through her Private Secretary – effectively the senior executive director – but all the administration and management of the business of monarchy come under the Lord Chamberlain. He has a white stave of office, which he breaks over the grave if his sovereign dies before him. (In fact it is made in two halves and he ceremonially unscrews it; he does not throw it into the grave – he is more likely to take it home as a souvenir.)

Footmen at a serving station during the Polish state banquet. The
scarlet and gold livery is an eighteenth-century pattern. There are
300 staff altogether on duty for a state banquet.
OPPOSITE In a room near St George's Hall, a chef prepares
the dessert for the Polish state banquet. The meal started with
quails' eggs, followed by turbot, veal with wild mushrooms, and
peaches Toscane.
OVERLEAF Laying the table for the state banquet for the President
of Poland. Places are measured with a ruler; with 160 guests you
do not want to get to the end of the table with four settings left and
nowhere to put them.

Upstairs the guests see what they are supposed to see – the liveried footmen,
the candelabra, the gold cutlery and silver gilt plates (silver gilt shines more
lustrously than gold; the pudding and dessert of fresh fruit are served on
china). 'Downstairs' it is more like a military operation than a theatrical
performance. For a typical Buckingham Palace banquet the stage will have
been set, so to speak, several hours before dinner and will have been personally inspected by the Queen late in the afternoon. Every place setting is
measured with a ruler, not from an obsession with precision, but because if

The Deputy Yeoman of the Royal Cellars decants the Dow 1966
port for the Polish state banquet. The 160 guests were also served
a 1985 hock, a 1979 claret and a 1985 champagne.
OPPOSITE All ready for the Polish state banquet in St George's
Hall, Windsor. The table is 160 feet long, more than two cricket
pitches. The cutlery is gold, the plates are silver gilt. Some of the
damask tablecloths on the serving tables are over 100 years old.

you do not do this you are liable to find yourself at the end of a 160-foot-long
table with four places to lay and nowhere to put them. 800 Stourbridge
crystal glasses engraved with the Queen's monogram will have been polished
and set. The parquet floor will have been covered with red carpet. Damask
tablecloths, some of them more than a century old, will have been brought
up from the basement linen room on wheeled trolleys. Men will have been
clambering on to the table tops to position the candelabra and the heavy
ornamental gold plate. A stream of vans will have been arriving at the
Pimlico side of the Palace delivering fresh bread, flowers, vegetables and
dairy produce. At 7.45 p.m. on the eve of the banquet the 'downstairs' staff
will have been given their final twenty-two-point briefing – they will be
reminded that Under Butlers serve potatoes only, that Wine Butlers will
serve the gravy, that Pantry Assistants will take away dirty dishes and cutlery

through the East Gallery, Silk Tapestry Room and service lift, and that the Plate Pantry Yeoman will instruct an Under Butler to warn the Palace Steward when the food is up and ready.

The dinner will proceed in ignorance of all this frantic activity. For the Polish state visit dinner began with quail's eggs, followed by turbot, with veal and wild mushrooms for the main course and peaches Toscane for pudding. A 1985 hock was served with the fish, a 1979 claret with the veal, vintage champagne with the pudding, and a 1966 port with the fruit and nuts. The Irish Guards band played a dozen numbers including Schubert, Haydn, Sousa and Cole Porter, and finally the pipe band of the Scots Guards marched round playing a Strathspey, a reel and two marches. After the meal, pages and footmen served coffee to the guests in the White Drawing-Room and the Green Drawing-Room. (Incidentally, on special occasions a footman walks down the corridor swinging a censer full of smouldering lavender.)

The washing-up and putting away went on long after the guests had gone to bed. You do not rush your way through 150 settings of priceless Minton china or chuck it in the dishwasher, and every piece of plate and cutlery has to be checked in as carefully as it was checked out by the Yeoman of the Gold and Silver Pantry. At one state banquet a gold fork went missing, causing major panic and the beginning of hideous suspicions about staff and even, in some unworthy breasts, about guests; but it was found in one of the rubbish bins with the left-over food.

Another unvarying ritual of state visits is the exchange of presents and decorations directly after lunch on the day of the state banquet. The Queen gave President Walesa the Grand Cross of the Order of the Bath and Collar, a pair of silver-framed photographs of herself and the Duke of Edinburgh, and a seventeenth-century map of Poland by John Speed. She gave Mrs Walesa a bound facsimile of the *Sobieski Book of Hours*. There was also an engraved carriage clock for the President and Mrs Walesa. In return the Walesas gave the Queen and the Duke of Edinburgh the Grand Ribbon of

The Queen with President Walesa of Poland in the Grand Reception Room before going in to the state banquet in Windsor Castle. This was the sixty-fifth state visit to Britain during the Queen's reign.

job. State visits may further the government's policies, but politically the Queen is an instrument and not an agent. Nevertheless, the fact that she is Head of State but not involved in politics gives her an interesting and important, though passive, role in one of the permanent private conflicts within government.

Officially, of course, there are no conflicts; the government is a single institution administering the nation's affairs. In practice, of course, it is like any other huge bureaucracy, a loose confederation of warring tribes. And of all the great departments of state it is the Foreign and Commonwealth Office, the FCO, that is the most likely to come into conflict with the government of the day. To the FCO relationships between countries are complex and sensitive. They have a long history and expect a long future. Today's opponents may be tomorrow's allies, and vice versa. There is good and bad in all regimes, the FCO believe, but we have to share a single world with all of them. More can be achieved quietly and privately than in the glare of publicity, and so on. All these are reasonable attitudes, even if not always and everywhere appropriate, but none of them is likely to bring an audience to its feet for a standing ovation. We who form the electorate want the big, understandable simplicities; we want goodies and baddies, and we can live quite happily with the confusion of changing them around within a few weeks, as for example with Iraq and Iran in 1990. We respond to leaders who speak out for Britain and pour scorn and defiance, slight regard, contempt and general abuse on our 'enemy' of the moment. We want to be told what is going on. And the more vigorously and stridently our politicians respond to our emotional needs, the more the diplomats in the FCO grit their teeth. 10 Downing Street is only a few feet away from the FCO geographically, but there have been times when they have been worlds apart politically. There are stories of spectacular rows.

There can be no doubt that constitutionally the Foreign Office ultimately has no alternative but to carry out the instructions of the government. They are, however, expert at endlessly postponing the ultimate, and one of their most powerful weapons – even if it can rarely be used – is the unspoken argument that they are servants of the state rather than the government. It has to be unspoken because it is for the government, not for diplomats, to decide what are the state's interests in foreign affairs. On the other hand, most politicians are fairly ignorant of foreign affairs and can be floored in

The Egyptian state visit, July 1991. President Mubarak talks to
the Queen Mother and Princess Margaret in the White Drawing-
Room at Buckingham Palace, before the State Banquet.

argument even by quite junior diplomats, if they were undiplomatic enough
to try. So, to distance themselves from the government of the day, the
FCO stress their relationship with the sovereign. The ambassadors are Her
Majesty's Ambassadors. They talk not about 'the government' but 'HMG' –
Her Majesty's Government. Not only is her portrait in every embassy usually
given massive prominence over the Prime Minister's; the national day cele-
brated abroad is neither a national event like Independence Day or Bastille
Day, nor any of our patron saints' days, but the Queen's Birthday. Every
new ambassador has a private audience with the Queen before going to take
up his post.

State visits emphasize the Queen's role as Head of State and at the same
time help to underline the fact that the Queen's relationship with the FCO
is extremely close. Although constitutionally it is the Home Secretary who
is historically the monarch's secretary, the Palace in fact does more business
with the FCO than with any other government department, more even than
with 10 Downing Street. Like so much else in the Queen's role in government,
this relationship cannot stop the implementation of declared government

Queen's is coded in yellow and marked 'The Queen'. The system is foolproof, but not souvenir-hunter proof, so the Travelling Yeoman always carries a supply of spare yellow labels. But even the most detailed planning can be frustrated: on the 1973 visit to Yugoslavia the Queen arrived in Dubrovnik to an empty airport. The reception committee had been told the flight was being diverted to Titograd, so there was no one to greet her when she landed. There was, however, a whole delegation waiting at Titograd with no one to greet.

The Queen's arrival in Washington for the 1991 state visit to the USA, where she was welcomed by President Bush on the White House lawn. The speaking lectern was too high for the cameras, so the world's television audience saw the Queen's hat better than her face.

A state visit is not a sort of holiday. The routine work of the monarchy goes on at the same time. The regular flow of Foreign Office telegrams, cabinet and Commonwealth papers, and press résumés still arrives every day, and the Queen has to pack black clothes for mourning and black-edged condolence stationery in case of a sudden death while she is away. Between thirty and fifty people accompany the Queen on a state visit; about a third are officials concerned with the business of the monarchy, and the rest are support staff – secretarial, security, dressers, hairdressers, and general management of the logistics and mechanics of the visit.

Not all royal visits are a success, as anyone who accompanied the Queen to Morocco in 1980 will tell you, but the American visit was so tumultuous that it almost embarrassed some of their press commentators. They had to coin a new word to describe it: monarchomania. The only visible hitch was the welcoming speech on the White House lawn, where the lectern was too high and only the Queen's hat was visible to the television cameras while she spoke. Even this was turned to advantage when the Queen's oblique reference to it in her speech to Congress ('I hope you can all see me today') received a big laugh and a round of applause. There were 2,000 guests on the White House lawn, and even so tickets were like gold dust. Wherever there was a royal reception – Washington, Florida, Texas – leading Americans were prepared to kill to obtain an invitation.

Since the USA became an independent state by throwing out a British king, you might expect them to show a distinct coolness towards a British sovereign; and since they believe so keenly that everyone should have an equal chance to get to the top, it would also be reasonable to expect a certain hostility to such a symbol of privilege and hierarchy as a hereditary monarch. Why then do so many Americans go mad about the British Royal Family? Perhaps it is because to a nation of restless and relentless upward strivers the Royal Family represents a social pinnacle which cannot be climbed by any native politician with a maximum eight-year term. Everest is still Everest even if it is in someone else's country. It is hard not to feel that somewhere

OVERLEAF Two days after her arrival in Washington the Queen addressed both houses of Congress. Her first words were, 'I hope you can all see me today.' Congress dissolved in laughter.

IN GOD WE TRUST

inside every democratic American there is a niggling regret at having thrown out the royal baby with the colonial bath water. It is almost as if they are searching for their own hereditary presidents – but Roosevelts and Kennedys make too many political enemies on their way up to be symbols of national unity. America's national emotions seem to find their focus more easily in Hollywood than on Capitol Hill; the Oscar ceremony parades the people whom Americans come to love and respect through the years and indeed the generations, and whose job is to make no enemies. Shirley Temple and Mickey Rooney are still remembered long after their political contemporaries like Calvin Coolidge and Herbert Hoover are forgotten. The two worlds only came together once, in Ronald Reagan, but it was a brief encounter and it does not seem to have added up to a substitute for monarchy.

The Washington visit was, of course, helped by a happy accident of timing. Britain became very popular in the USA because of her immediate and wholehearted support of the American action in the Gulf War, and the visit some three months later gave all concerned a topical theme to reinforce ideas of a special relationship and a shared commitment to freedom and democracy. Ideas like these still have the power to make many people feel warm inside, back in Britain as well as in America. There is, however, one aspect of the Queen's 'outward' role as Head of State that requires far more delicate footsteps, and while she was in the USA preparations were going ahead for its great biennial event: the Commonwealth Heads of Government meeting in Zimbabwe from 16 to 22 October 1991.

All the rest of the Queen's roles as Head of State are ancient, but Head of the Commonwealth is certainly modern: the concept of a British Commonwealth of Nations was thought up by Lord Balfour in the year the Queen was born, 1926, to explain the status of independent states like Australia and Canada who were not subjects of the British Empire but who kept the British

OPPOSITE ABOVE HMY *Britannia* anchored in Tampa Bay, Florida, during the 1991 state visit to the USA. The *Britannia* provides the Royal party with a secure home base and office during foreign visits and a place to return their hosts' hospitality.
After dinner on HMY *Britannia*, the Queen's guests are treated to a display of Beating the Retreat on the quayside at Miami, Florida, during the 1991 state visit to the USA.

The special relationship: the Queen and President Reagan go
for a ride in the grounds of Windsor Castle during the
US state visit in 1982.
OPPOSITE The Princess of Wales talks to Barbara Bush, wife of
the US President, at a Buckingham Palace reception for the 'G7'
heads of state and government at the London economic
summit in July 1991.

President Bush and Lord Callaghan of Cardiff meet again at
Buckingham Palace during the 1991 'G7' economic summit in
London. While James Callaghan was Prime Minister (1976–79),
George Bush was director of the CIA.
OPPOSITE Firework display at Buckingham Palace after the dinner
for the heads of state and government at the London 'G7' summit,
July 1991. The massed band of the combined services played
Handel's 'Music for the Royal Fireworks'. Organizers of
international conferences devoutly hope that these will be the only
kind of fireworks during the proceedings.

sovereign as their own. In another sense, though, it did not begin until 1949,
when India arranged to become a republic but stay within the 'Commonwealth'. This not only changed the nature of the Commonwealth; it also
gave the British sovereign a completely new kind of role as head of an
organization whose members owed no allegiance to the Crown and might
be hostile to or even, in theory, at war with the United Kingdom.

It is really quite difficult to discover what the Commonwealth is for. It has
been described as the most civilized method yet discovered for dismantling an
empire, and indeed it is easier to explain in terms of how it happened than
what it does. It came into being because the great majority of the countries

Sydney residents welcome 'Australia's Queen' during bicentenary
celebrations in May 1988.
OPPOSITE The Queen, accompanied by Sir Eric Neal, is shown the
statue of Queen Victoria in Sydney; it was a gift from the Irish
government in honour of the country's bicentenary.
OVERLEAF The Queen addresses the Commonwealth heads of
government at a state dinner during the 1989 Commonwealth
Conference in Kuala Lumpur, Malaysia. They represent between a
quarter and a third of the world's population.

in the British Empire did not want to lose all connection with Britain and each other when they became independent. In that sense it is a sort of old comrades association. Now that it is there, it acts as a curious informal forum which brings together a multiracial group of heads of government of something between a quarter and a third of the world's population (though if India left, the figure would drop dramatically) for a reunion meeting every two years.

Its members come from all the world's main groupings except the Middle East: Europe, Asia, North and South America, Africa, the Caribbean, the Pacific and Australasia, and although it is an association of equal sovereign

Canada's National Day, 1 July 1990: The Governor-General of
Canada applauds the Queen's speech in Ottawa.

states, the only thread that binds them all together is Britain, and Britain is represented and personified by the Queen, who is also Queen of seventeen of its fifty member countries. She is not only the Head of the Commonwealth, she is also its longest serving member; no other head of government or member of the secretariat can match her forty years of continuous service. She has seen colonies change into self-governing states; protectorates change into monarchies; dominions change into republics; parliamentary democracies change into police states and back again. She has seen constitutions altered, coups succeed and fail, politicians come and go, heads of state be deposed, assassinated and superseded. She has a private one-to-one audience with every head of government at each biennial meeting, but the job is a continuous one. Every day she receives, as their Queen, confidential news briefs from Australia, Canada and New Zealand, and Commonwealth business takes up a considerable amount of her time.

Is it all worth it? Certainly there are those who would like to see the Queen abandon this role and who would regard the break-up of the Commonwealth as no great loss. They see it as a pointless talking shop whose purpose is to pressurize the British Government into actions that benefit other Commonwealth countries at the expense of the British people; and quite often the words and deeds of other Commonwealth governments on issues like sanctions against South Africa arouse hostile emotions in Britain that go deeper than public speeches and leading newspaper articles. Others believe it is a unique forum for a wide group of very different nations who share a common historical link, and that it gives Britain a special importance and influence in world affairs. Both cases can be argued, but, as long as the argument goes on, the role of Head of the Commonwealth is one the Queen has to exercise with extreme delicacy and discretion.

5

THE FOUNT OF HONOUR

On Saturday 4 May 1991 hundreds, perhaps thousands, of British citizens took a final disappointed look at their morning's post and then resigned themselves to waiting for another six months.

The importance of the date is that it was six weeks before the Queen's official birthday on 15 June (her actual birthday is on 21 April). On that day the list of birthday honours is published in the *London Gazette,* and also in *The Times, Daily Telegraph* and *Guardian,* but no one's name is included if they have not already been approached and indicated that they are happy to accept the offered award. A typical letter will run like this:

The Prime Minister has asked me to inform you in strict confidence that he has it in mind on the occasion of the forthcoming list of birthday honours to submit your name to the Queen with the recommendation that Her Majesty be graciously pleased to approve that you be appointed an Officer of the Order of the British

ABOVE Sir Brian Goswell being knighted by the Queen. After being touched on each shoulder by the sword he has a brief conversation with the Queen before bowing, taking four paces backwards, bowing again and turning right to leave the Ballroom. The ribbon and medal are put in a presentation box for him by a clerk.

Empire. Before doing so, the Prime Minister would be glad to be assured that this would be agreeable to you.

The letter always arrives at least six weeks before the Queen's Birthday or New Year's Day so, once that date has passed, hopes have to be put off. Some of those approached do indeed refuse. Graham Greene refused a knighthood (though he later became a Companion of Honour) and Evelyn Waugh refused a CBE, saying that he would prefer to wait until he won his spurs, but the Palace never discloses the names of those who refuse. What is no secret is that the vast majority hasten to assure the Prime Minister that it would be agreeable to them, even if they are as anti-establishment as the Beatles or Vanessa Redgrave.

Britain is not the only country which bestows honours on its citizens, but no other country in the world does it through a system that is so ancient – antiquated, if you like – varied, complex and wide-ranging. There are nine orders of chivalry dating back to the Order of the Garter, which was founded in 1348, and many have different classes within them: the largest of all, the Order of the British Empire has five plus a medal – GBE, KBE, CBE, OBE, MBE and BEM, which is quite impressive since there is in fact no British Empire left. There are some 100,000 living members of the order, and its register, which includes the dead as well as the living, has more than half a million names on it. Every six months something like 1,000 people are honoured and, although the names come from 10 Downing Street or other offices of state, they are all technically bestowed by the Queen, who is the 'fount of honour'. In fact some 700 of those 1,000 six-monthly honours are more than technically bestowed: the Queen personally fastens the medal on the breast or hangs the ribbon round the neck or drapes the sash over the shoulder at every one of the fifteen annual investiture ceremonies. The other 300 are recipients of the British Empire Medal, whose award is presented on the Queen's behalf by her local representative, the Lord Lieutenant of their

OVERLEAF Cleaning the East Gallery at Buckingham Palace
ready for an investiture ceremony. Honours are
announced twice a year: on New Year's Day and on the
Queen's official birthday which is usually the second Saturday
in June. Her real birthday is 21 April.

103

county – a distinction which drew a sharp letter of protest in *The Times* in January 1991 from a recipient who saw it as a sign of class discrimination.

Creating or reinforcing class discrimination is only one of the regular criticisms of the honours system. It is also accused of rewarding too many public officials for little more than doing what they are paid to do and hanging on for twenty years without getting caught with their hands in the till, and too few selfless unpaid charity workers who lack the patronage of an important institution. It is accused of being used as a political publicity gimmick, as an encouragement to contribute to party funds, and as a cheap way to pension off party hacks or soften the blow of sacking. Every now and then someone calls for the whole system to be radically reformed or abolished. And yet it goes on year after year, or half-year after half-year, with undiminished interest from the press and eagerness from the recipients.

Anyone can in theory recommend anyone for an honour simply by writing to the Prime Minister. In practice any recommendation that is to have a chance will need some form of establishment support – for instance a Lord Lieutenant, an MP, a top civil servant or the head of a large institution preferably, but not necessarily, public or charitable. Some 3,000 recommendations arrive each half-year in the office of the Appointments Secretary in 10 Downing Street. They are scrutinized by secret committees of experts. Names recommended for honours in the arts and sciences, say, will have been through a committee of senior men and women from the arts and science establishment. The system used to be much more informal until politicians – Lloyd George in particular – started to use it for blatant party fund-raising. The committees are there as a safeguard against the sale of honours and, although the Prime Minister can override their decision, it would cause raised eyebrows and discreet enquiries as to his reasons for doing so.

Certain honours are the personal gift of the Queen – the Orders of the Garter and the Thistle and the Royal Victorian Order, for instance, or the Order of Merit (which she bestowed on Margaret Thatcher on her resignation in November 1990) – but the vast majority of recipients are simply names suggested by others such as the Prime Minister, the Foreign Office and the armed services. The list is submitted to the Queen twice, once for informal approval and the second time for formal approval. If she wanted to question any of the recommendations, she would do so at the informal

The Comptroller of the Lord Chamberlain's Office (*right*) and
Lieutenant-General Sir Peter Graham at a briefing session for
recipients of honours just before an investiture. There are fifteen
investiture ceremonies every year.

stage. It is never revealed whether the Queen crosses any names off the list
once it reaches the Palace, but it is generally understood that she could
if she wanted. Previous monarchs have been known to refuse to honour
homosexuals or adulterers. So, although the Queen does not personally select
most of the recipients of honours, they do have the comforting knowledge
that at least she did not reject them.

It is very rare for honours to be withdrawn, but it happens: Anthony Blunt was stripped of his knighthood in November 1979 after being revealed as a traitor, and on 27 March 1991 Jack Lyons lost his after he was found guilty in the Guinness fraud trial. There was a special irony about Anthony Blunt's treason since he was a Knight Commander of the Victorian Order (KCVO), awarded for personal services to the sovereign – he had been Surveyor of the Queen's Pictures. Not every conviction by the courts leads to loss of honours: recipients can survive a parking fine or even a brief spell in jail, but they would be pushing their luck if they got themselves sent down for more than three months. Sometimes it happens the other way round, and recipients return their medals in protest; several were returned in this way at the start of the Gulf War. But once an honour has been bestowed, it belongs to the recipient for ever, so returned medals and decorations are kept at the Central Chancery of the Orders of Knighthood in case the owners ask for them back later. They quite often do so, and the insignia are returned to them in the same box and wrapping paper in which they were sent.

The lists of honours to be given are prepared in the deepest secrecy. 300 copies have to be printed, but the Assistant Secretary of the Central Chancery checks all the proofs personally – clerks and secretaries never see them – and Macauley's Press is a part of Her Majesty's Stationery Office with security systems developed for protecting all the Budget documents. After the announcement, letters are sent out to the recipients summoning (not inviting) them to their investiture. They are asked if they are able to kneel, so that if they are in a wheelchair arrangements can be made, and under what name they wish to be officially honoured. There will be no problems with abbreviations like Ted or Peggy, but you might be asked to think again if you chose to be called Dame Bubbles or Sir Bobbity.

The Chancery also has to make the physical arrangements. Their vaults are like wine cellars, with the various medals and insignia stored together in their sections. A gold collar for a grand order can cost about £66,000, though it is only on loan to the recipient; but he or she keeps the badge and star, which cost £3,000. At the other end of the scale, the MBE badge costs £45, but the BEM, a lower order, costs £4 more because it has the holder's name engraved on it.

All the insignia in correct order of precedence are arranged on trays on the tables in the Ballroom at Buckingham Palace. The Queen does not have to worry about the organization of it all, but she always studies briefing notes on all the hundred or more recipients before the ceremony. In fact the platform arrangements are very like an extremely high-class version of a school prizegiving, with great care taken to see that nobody gets someone else's prize. Even so mistakes can be made. Lord Chamberlains have been known to miss a line and call a name out of turn, so the officials on the platform have to stay alert for last-second changes in the batting order.

Recipients are booked in and given a briefing on what they have to do: MBEs and gallantry medal recipients in the right-hand wing of the Picture Gallery, CBEs and OBEs in the left, and knights in the Green Drawing-Room. If they are to kneel, they can practise with a replica kneeling stool. This is where unusual pronunciations of names are detected and passed to the Lord Chamberlain and the platform. If they are to receive a medal, a small hook is fastened to their lapel or dress for the Queen to hang the award on, rather than jabbing in a pin. The staff who book recipients in are called bookers; the staff who hook people up are not called hookers. At the ceremony itself

The insignia ready for presentation by the Queen. Britain has the most ancient and complex honours system in the world. There are nine orders of chivalry and many of them have several classes. The largest is the Order of the British Empire, with 100,000 members.

friends and relations sit in the Ballroom – there will be 200 or so of them – the band plays selections from Gilbert and Sullivan or other appropriate light music, and the recipients queue up in an annexe outside the Ballroom, and go up in turn as their names are called. They receive the honour, talk for twenty or thirty seconds to the Queen, take four paces backwards, bow, turn right and walk out. As they reach the door, a clerk unhooks the medal, puts it in a presentation box and gives it back to them. The whole ceremony

The Assistant Comptroller of the Lord Chamberlain's Office checks the insignia before the ceremony. An investiture is like a school prizegiving – it is important to ensure that no one gets the wrong award.

lasts for one hour and ten minutes. After forty years of investitures the Queen has probably bestowed honours on something like 80,000 or 90,000 different people, but for almost all the recipients it is a once-in-a-lifetime experience.

The honours system is not the chief means by which the Queen maintains her role as Head of the Nation, but it is the most obvious, the most publicized and the most formal. Together with the peerage, it forms the national status system and, since only about a dozen new peers are created each year – and they are not invested by the Queen, but 'introduced' into the House of Lords by existing peers – it is the six-monthly honours list that is by far the more important element.

There is a fashionable view that status-seeking and status displays are in some way undesirable or unworthy, but the truth is that status is universal to our species and to every species of social animal. You can choose what sort of system you will have, but you cannot choose *not* to have one. The comrades who founded the Soviet Union swept away all the ranks and privileges of the Tsars, but a new system grew up which was every bit as subtle and pervasive as the one it replaced. The privileges of the *nomenklatura*, the inner group of the Communist Party, were as significant as those of the court of the Romanovs. Canada decided to abandon the British honours system as an undemocratic anachronism, but soon realized the need for something to replace it and invented the Order of Canada complete with companions, officers and members. Badges of status are visible all over the world and in every walk of life: very obviously in the armed forces, for example, but no less clearly, if you know where to look, in the modern corporation. Managers do not wear pips or stripes or medals, but their status is affirmed in dozens of different ways: the car they drive or in which they are driven, the place where they park it; the size of their office, the floor level it is on, the quality of furnishing, whether they share it with another manager or their secretary, or have no secretary, or three in an outside office; where they eat and wash, whether they have flowers in the office and a drinks cabinet, a butler, porcelain tea service or vending machine in the corridor, and a hundred other subtle distinctions and gradations. People will tell you these are all operational or commercial necessities, and of course a few of them are, but most are not. In the civil service a certain seniority level used to entitle a manager to a wall-to-wall office carpet; if a junior moved in to the office, someone had to come and turn the carpet back two inches all round the room.

Status is one of the ways a species keeps order. If everyone knows their place, internal squabbles are avoided. Often the order has to be established by squabbles but, once it is fixed, peace can reign and discipline can be maintained. It is no coincidence that the word 'order' has three meanings: first a command, second a pecking order, and third the opposite of chaos. Nor is it a coincidence that the different kinds of honour are called 'orders'.

Almost everyone of us has a place in one status system or another; many of us belong in several different ones. As well as work status systems, the corporate hierarchy, there are professional status systems – medical, legal, educational; regional systems – borough and county councils; sporting systems – from the world champion to the newest club member; leisure group systems, charity systems, trades union systems; in fact there are status systems for every form of organized human activity. Most of them have some form of status display – a title (doctor, councillor, hon. treasurer), a uniform, a badge, a cap, a privilege within the group, a special room, a special place at the table, a chain of office, name printed on writing paper or painted on the honours board of past presidents. All of them signify some special achievement, contribution or importance within the group. All of them demonstrate some form of recognition by the rest of the group.

The British honours system does no more than this. Indeed it does rather less, since none of the twice-yearly honours carries with it any duties or responsibilities. Its main difference is that it is not regional, professional or occupational – it is national. It brings together people from central and local government, business, sport, the arts, the armed forces, the voluntary organizations, education, science, etc., from all over the United Kingdom, into a single national status system with the Queen at the head of it. No one could pretend that it has much active effect on the life of the nation, but it plays its part in creating a feeling of a national community focused on the sovereign. Only 2,000 people a year receive honours out of a nation of more than fifty-seven million. Even so, that means that some 80,000 will have been honoured by the Queen during her reign, and they will all have friends, neighbours, relatives and colleagues. It also makes a statement: even if people on the list are not actually chosen by the Queen, they are presumed to be

Lord Whitelaw robing up as a Knight of the Thistle in the Signet
Library for the Knights of the Thistle procession into St Giles
Cathedral, Edinburgh, in July 1991. The Thistle is one of the orders
in the personal gift of the sovereign.

the sort of people and be doing the sort of job that the nation respects and
values. They will, of course, include the usual quota of generals, ambassadors
and senior civil servants, but also – to quote from a recent list – people such
as a dust suppression officer with British Coal from Yorkshire, a lady from
Egham who rescues swans, a village baker from Penshurst in Kent, and a
travelling ticket inspector from Wolverhampton.

What is harder, in fact impossible, to measure is the effect of the system
on those who do not have honours, but are hoping for them – the ones who
are disappointed by the morning mail six weeks before the Queen's Birthday
and New Year's Day. How many senior figures take on unpaid public
responsibilities in the hope that their public-spiritedness will be recognized?
How many wealthy tycoons decide to support worthy causes? How many
industrial magnates take or refrain from taking business decisions in order
not to damage their chances next time round? Or, for that matter, how many
senior civil servants avoid any enterprising initiatives in case they backfire

at exactly the wrong moment? For most citizens the honours list may be at most an amusing irrelevance, but as people climb higher up their chosen tree it occupies an ever larger place in their imagination.

And what does it all achieve? Certainly it makes a small number of people very happy and proud, and perhaps a slightly larger number envious, resentful or derisive; for every appointment there are always ten disappointments. But is it worth all the trouble? Probably many of those who do not go so far as to call for its abolition still see it as little more than a bit of harmless nonsense. Politically they have a very good case; to all intents and purposes the honours system has nothing to do with the process of government. To abolish the House of Lords would cause a massive constitutional convulsion, but, if honours were abolished tomorrow, the government of the United Kingdom would continue without even a hiccup. The peerage is one of the ingredients of the constitutional cake; honours are merely the icing on it.

To understand the place of the honours system in the Queen's job it is necessary to see her role as in fact two roles, Head of the State and Head of the Nation. As Head of the State her role is well understood and clearly defined: Parliament has to be opened, Orders in Council have to be approved, Acts of Parliament have to be signed, ambassadors have to be accredited, visiting heads of state have to be greeted and entertained. But she is also Head of the Nation. That half of her job is nothing like so clearly defined, but this does not make it any less important or less interesting.

The duties of the Head of State are laid down by law and confirmed by time and custom, but there is no law that makes the Head of State also the Head of Nation. A nation is a cultural but not necessarily a legal unit. A nation does not have to accept the head of state as its natural leader, its tribal chieftain, as during 1991 the Kurdish nation did not accept the President of Iraq as theirs. The people of Britain did not look to George I,

The Queen in the robes of a Knight of the Garter for the Garter procession to St George's Chapel, Windsor, in June 1991. The Garter is the oldest order of chivalry, dating back to 1348, and, like the Thistle, is personally awarded by the sovereign. There are twenty-four Knights Companion.

when he arrived from Hanover in 1714 unable to speak more than a few words of English, as leader of the nation, even though they accepted him as head of state. He was a legitimate descendant of the royal line and not a Roman Catholic, and those two facts were enough to remove any serious objections to his inheriting the crown; but they did not mean that the people of Britain looked to him as a symbol of Britishness or as the embodiment of the nation's virtues and values in the way they might have looked to someone like the great military leader the Duke of Marlborough. Even 100 years later the far more English George IV could not claim the level of affection and respect that his subjects gave to that other famous general, the Duke of Wellington, after he had won the Battle of Waterloo. And to come closer to the present time, the fact that some of the people of Northern Ireland do not accept the Queen as head of their nation, or identify with the British national culture, creates a far greater level of instability there than anywhere else in the kingdom.

Nevertheless it seems clear that a nation – any nation – wants its head of state to be the natural leader of the nation as well. With every new President the people of the United States look to the White House for a lead in manners and morals as well as in politics and government, but the relatively short time he is in power and the fact that the President necessarily has many political opponents makes the role much harder for him to sustain than it is for a king or queen. This American national need is often overlooked by political commentators who tend to be baffled by the continuing popularity of someone they believe to have been a political failure – Eisenhower, say, or Reagan – because they underestimate the strength of the national need for a tribal chieftain and the skill of the President in establishing himself as a successful head of the nation even when informed commentators agree he has been an unsuccessful head of the administration.

The strength of this collective human need was very clearly demonstrated by the surge of national emotion for the eighteen-year-old Queen Victoria in 1837 after the last of her uncles died, and she did indeed become accepted as Head of the Nation in her people's eyes well before the end of her reign; the British Royal Family have continued in that role ever since.

It is not, however, a role that can be taken for granted; indeed it trembled in the balance in 1936 during Edward VIII's abdication crisis, though it was firmly restored by the behaviour of the Royal Family in the Second World

War. But as long as the sovereign is accepted as the true head of the people, the state has a stability that it would not have otherwise. The honours system plays a significant, though not crucial, part in that process. But an event in April 1991 symbolized a much older and, in its day, a much more important instrument for welding the state and nation together.

On 15 April 1991 George Carey, the new Archbishop of Canterbury, went to Windsor Castle to do homage to the Queen before being enthroned at Canterbury Cathedral four days later. The constitutional significance of this act is immense, but for practical purposes today it is largely historical. In the Middle Ages the Catholic Church was the focus of loyalty for the people of England, but it was ultimately answerable to the Pope in Rome and not to the King in London. The Archbishop's homage reaffirms the Church's acceptance of Henry VIII's Reformation in 1534, by which he in effect nationalized the Church (and seized many of its assets). This act had endless military, political and theological consequences, but one of its effects was to join together the state and the nation in a way that had never been possible before. It released a great surge of patriotism under Elizabeth I (1558–1603), which was made stronger by memories of the reign of terror under Mary Tudor from 1553 to 1558 and the threat of invasion in 1588 by Philip II and the Spanish Armada to reclaim England for the Pope.

The first Elizabethan Age was a high point of unity between nation and state, and the established church (the Church of England) was the principal instrument of unity. It was a very powerful instrument; if you were a true believer then to challenge the legal right of the government was not just treachery but heresy as well. It was nevertheless one of those instruments like the nuclear bomb that only works as long as you do not have to use it. When Charles I tried to assert his royal and divine authority in 1642, the result was a disaster. The nation was split in two by a bloody civil war, and in the end the whole apparatus of state was overthrown and Oliver Cromwell and the Puritans had to invent a new one.

OVERLEAF The Queen with her new Archbishop of Canterbury.
Dr George Carey went to Windsor Castle to do homage to the
Queen on 15 April 1991 before his enthronement in Canterbury
Cathedral on 19 April.

The Queen with the new Archbishop of Canterbury in the library
of Windsor Castle during a 'dine and sleep' visit in April 1991.
Bishops and archbishops are appointed by the Queen, but in practice
she has to follow the recommendation of the Prime Minister.
OPPOSITE As Supreme Governor of the Church of England, the
Queen opens its General Synod in November 1990. Before the
Reformation, the Pope in Rome was head of the Church in England.
Since 1534 the British sovereign has been the supreme head.

The Civil War, 1642–48, changed the entire relationship between the
Crown and the government, but it also changed the relationship between
the state and the nation. The Church of England, which was meant to be
the focus and expression of the whole nation's religious belief and devotion,
never again reached the peak of popularity it did under Elizabeth I. By the
1800s it had become known as the Tory Party at prayer. Break-away church
movements like Methodism grew hand in hand with trade unionism as
organizations of patriotic British citizens who did not identify with the
government. It was a period of deep unrest: the Gordon Riots, Peterloo, the
Reform Bill, Chartism and the Corn Laws were not just matters for political

debate, they were feared as potential causes of bloody revolution. The state and the nation were dangerously far apart, and did not start to come together again until the second half of the nineteenth century.

It may all seem very long ago now, but monarchy is a long-term business, and political stability is slow to build, but quick to crumble as the Soviet Union found in August 1991. The established church cannot create national unity on its own – indeed has not been able to for several centuries. In 1991 only some 3% of the British people regularly attended Church of England services. None the less, the fact that it is established is not without influence even on the other 97%. Its decisions are taken as in some way expressing Britain's moral code. If it decides to accept women or self-declared homosexuals into the priesthood, non-churchgoers feel somehow involved in the decision in a way they would not if it were a decision by the Catholic or Methodist Churches: the Church of England may not be 'their' church, but their Queen is its supreme head, so somehow they feel it speaks for them even if they do not believe in God and never attend its services. Being Head of the Church does not automatically turn the sovereign into the accepted Head of the Nation, but it adds a moral and spiritual dimension to the Crown, as if the Queen were somehow the official trustee of the national standards of right and wrong in a way that few presidents of republics would claim to be. To say that the Queen would not approve of some form of conduct is a much more serious criticism than to say that President Bush or President Mitterrand would not approve of it. And for most British citizens it would be a more serious criticism than saying that the Archbishop of Canterbury would not approve of it.

For over a century British kings and queens have given out a stream of signals of approval and disapproval, by the guests they have received, the events they have attended, the people they have honoured, the charities they have supported, the countries they have visited, and even the ways they have spent their leisure. Their disapproval has been shown more by what they have not done, like not honouring divorcees or homosexuals. The British public would expect to see the Queen at a race meeting, but would be shocked if she spent her spare time in a casino. Indeed you could almost define British moral standards by listing everything that the British would be shocked or disappointed to find the Queen doing, even if they habitually did it themselves. This moral trusteeship extends to all the Royal Family. If the daughter of a cousin of the President of the United States conceived a child out of wedlock, it would hardly make the local papers, but in 1990 Marina Ogilvy was the lead story in the national press and stayed in the headlines for weeks.

This British acceptance of the Queen as an arbiter of right and wrong goes well beyond serious moral issues at the level of the Ten Commandments and the Sermon on the Mount. It extends into the niceties of good manners and correct behaviour. Many of today's parents when they were children were regularly corrected with a phrase like, 'You wouldn't do that in front of the Queen, would you?' People write to the Palace to ask if a married friend should be addressed as 'Mrs John Smith' or 'Mrs Mary Smith' (the Palace does not issue rules of etiquette; they just say that 'Mrs John Smith' is the form they use, but that is good enough for most people). The sovereign is accepted as the ultimate arbiter of the minutiae of table manners, dress for formal occasions and correct speech – the Queen's English. Again, this does not mean that everyone wants or tries to behave, dress and speak like the Queen; quite visibly most people do not. But it does mean that they accept that it is the standard form, even if they themselves have no desire or intention to comply with it.

To the British people, who have grown up with the idea of the sovereign as setting and exemplifying the national standard of moral and social behaviour, it all seems perfectly natural. In fact, of course, as we have seen, it was not always so and could easily cease to be so. The central role of the sovereign as Head of the Nation is to continue to fill that position, to continue being accepted as the leader in spirit as well as in law, thereby attaching to the state and the system of government the same British national emotions which are called forth by events like the World Cup and the Olympic Games. This will not ensure popularity for the government of the day: what it will ensure is that even the most unpopular government will still be accepted as being the Queen's government because it has the social as well as the constitutional force of the Crown behind it.

6

AWAYDAYS

Honours have a high profile. All awards and ratings create interest and argument – the Oscars, the Nobel Prizes, the Booker Prize – and one which distributes 2,000 a year across the nation is bound to be especially newsworthy. It is not, however, all that important a part of the Queen's job as Head of the Nation. The real work goes on day after day and year after year in a much less glamorous way.

At exactly 1.30 p.m. on Friday 30 November 1990 the Royal Train pulled in to Huddersfield station. Five local dignitaries were presented to the Queen. At 1.35 the royal party arrived at the headquarters of the British Amateur Rugby League Association. Five more people were presented, and the young daughters of two of them presented a posy to the Queen. She was then taken on a tour of the building, more people were presented, trophies were inspected, drinks were served, lunch was taken, a present was given, the loyal toast was drunk, the visitors' book was signed, and a plaque was unveiled. At 3.15 the Queen left by car. At 3.20 she arrived at Huddersfield Sports Centre. More presentations. Another bouquet. 3.25 view local paint-

ABOVE July 1991, the Queen visits the East of England Agricultural Show at Peterborough, another insight into the working life of the country.

The Queen on her way to the Palace of Holyroodhouse, Edinburgh,
by Intercity 225 in June 1991. The Queen holds an annual Garden
Party at Holyrood and carries out a week of engagements in Scotland.
OVERLEAF Intercity to Edinburgh – the Queen takes a break from
work to relax with her entourage.

ings; 3.30 view soft play area for handicapped children and activities for the over-fifties; 3.45 displays in sports hall; 4.00 p.m. four-year-olds in 'rough and tumble' junior gymnastics. Another plaque, another visitors' book. Leave at 4.15. 4.35 arrive at Claremont Retirement Home. Presentations, posies, plaques. Tea with residents, staff and volunteers. 5.35 leave by car for the station.

Saturday morning, 1 December, 10.10 a.m. (exactly) the Royal Train arrives at Gateshead. Inspect civic centre, open a new bridge, cut the ribbon for a new by-pass, tour Swan Hunter shipyards, launch a ship. Presentations, plaques, posies, presents; coffee, tea, receptions, lunch, loyal toasts. Leave Newcastle airport at 2.45 p.m. Back at Windsor at 4.10 p.m. and the end of another awayday.

Most of the Queen's official engagements are of necessity in London, where Parliament, government and embassies are based, but the Queen's realm extends beyond Whitehall and Westminster – even beyond Watford and Wimbledon. You can do the job of Head of State without moving outside the capital, but the Head of the Nation cannot be merely a metropolitan monarch. So about thirty times a year the Queen, with a party of some four or five people, goes on these visits to her subjects all around her kingdom. The Duke of Edinburgh goes out on about fifty visits. Their pattern does not change much, but each one takes a good deal of organizing.

The Queen visits around 150 organizations a year, but for any individual one of them it is almost certainly a unique event. Their pleasure is mixed with panic. What would the Queen like to see? Whom would she like to meet? How should she be addressed? How long should she spend touring the premises? Should we fly a flag? (Only if a vertical flagpole is available.) Do we provide toilet facilities? Who should sit next to her at lunch? Is there any food she can't eat or doesn't like? (Yes – oysters.) Indian or China tea? What flowers does the Queen like? (All flowers, but not wired bunches – she once cut her hand on a wired bouquet.) And apart from all these and a hundred other questions, there will be displays to rehearse, exhibitions to prepare,

A posy for the Queen during a birthday walkabout in Swansea in 1989. The Queen makes about thirty trips a year to visit different parts of her kingdom.

Belfast seen from the Queen's military escort helicopter during her
visit to Northern Ireland, June 1991. She landed at Lisburn barracks
and presented new colours to the Ulster Defence Regiment.

speeches to write, plaques to engrave, posies to arrange and an orgy of
painting, polishing, oiling, scrubbing, vacuum cleaning, repairing, reup-
holstering, dusting, tidying and generally making the place fit for a queen.
For those in charge it is an honour which borders on an ordeal.

Even so, it is nothing compared with the work that has to go into the visit
from the Palace end. Naturally there is not the same panic; it is not the first
time for the Palace staff as it is for the people they are visiting. None the less
you cannot relax when you are responsible for the safety of the Queen. A
typical visit will be fixed perhaps a year in advance and serious detailed
planning begins some twelve weeks before D-day, or Q-day. Virtually all
visits start with an invitation, though technically they are undertaken 'on
the advice of ministers'. Since the Queen receives many more invitations
than she can undertake, there has to be a winnowing process. Anything with
a hint of party political colouring goes out straight away. So does anything

that looks as if it is an attempt to use the royal visit as an advertising gimmick. If there is any political sensitivity about the visit, the Queen's Private Secretaries ask for advice from the Cabinet Secretary. They also have to check that the organization is not petitioning for bankruptcy or under investigation by the Fraud Squad, and that the chairman is not helping police with their enquiries. On the positive side, the organization needs to be in a reputable kind of business and to have a significant enough event to

The Queen talks to patients and staff at the Somerton House Hospice
in Belfast in June 1991. This was her first visit to Northern Ireland
since 1977.

The Queen at RAF Benson with the staff of The Queen's Flight.
Needless to say they are not all on the Queen's plane at the same
time. They are a group of regular serving airmen from whom a crew
will be chosen when the Queen needs them.
OPPOSITE Waving farewell, the Queen boards an aircraft of The
Queen's Flight at Aldergrove airport, Belfast, at the end of her visit,
which for security reasons was kept secret until the last minute.
OVERLEAF Scotland, August 1991, HMY *Britannia* anchored in Loch
Linnhe in the Great Glen during the Queen's visit to mark the
tercentenary of the burgh of Fort William.

celebrate. It will also help if it is in a part of the country the Queen has not
visited for some time or, alternatively, if it can be fitted in with a visit that
is already scheduled. Its type of activity will also count; visits to six light
bulb factories in the same month would clearly be overdoing things.

Once the selection has been made, the planning begins. There will, of
course, be briefings to give to the people the Queen will be visiting and
all their questions to answer. Not all the questions come from the actual

organization: for example, a gardener wrote to the Queen saying he could not afford a dark suit in which to be presented to her. The Palace replied that the Queen never stipulates the colour of clothes to be worn and 'any instructions issued locally should be regarded merely in the nature of guidance. Her Majesty never wishes people to be put to extra expense on account of her visits and would certainly not wish you specially to acquire for this occasion a suit of darker colour than the one you already possess.'

Some of the preparation cannot be done by post or telephone. One of her three Private Secretaries always reconnoitres the site personally well in advance of the Queen's visit. His local contact is the Lord Lieutenant of the county, who is the Queen's official representative in the area, and they will normally go over the ground together. The locations are checked, the route is precisely measured and timed, and if there are hazards like ladders, gangplanks or steep steps they are closely looked over; on some occasions male officials have to assess how practicable a complicated route is for the Queen. There is also a security check. The Queen is something of a security nightmare since she does not travel in armour-plated cars with bullet-proof windows, and it is in the nature of these visits that times and routes should be published well in advance, so the Palace security police and the local force do a full survey and policing schedule long before the visit.

Back at base, all the transport preparations have to be made, the detailed programme for the visit has to be agreed and circulated, and the Queen's wardrobe has to be chosen. The clothes will probably have been designed by Norman Hartnell or Hardy Amies, and she may possibly wear up to three different outfits in any given day. There is a strong practical element to the designers' brief: her clothes must be suitable for a lot of standing around and walking about, outdoors as well as indoors; skirts and hats must not be too vulnerable to gusts of wind; bright clothes help her to be seen by everyone; heavy coats look awkward when being put on and taken off; large hat brims conceal the Queen's face from people who have come a long way and waited a long time to see her; some outfits have to look dignified without being dowdy, others must be splendid without being flashy; handbags are generally black or white to go with anything; and umbrellas are transparent so that she can be seen in the rain. Gloves protect her hands from the endless handshakes – a Brighton firm has supplied literally hundreds of pairs of white gloves during the past forty years. There must also be spares for emergencies.

When Prince Charles was very small, he pressed a half-sucked boiled sweet into the Queen's gloved hand just as she was about to get out of the car and shake hands with the reception committee. The Lady-in-Waiting instantly produced a spare pair.

When it comes to the visit itself, the timing will be precise. If the timetable is overrun people will be kept waiting and some meetings will have to be dropped – meetings which people are likely to have been looking forward to for months and which for many of them would have been one of the high points of their lives; and, if the royal train is involved, late running can disrupt commuter services. So all the Palace party have miniature copies of

The Queen on the Royal Barge about to land at Fort William for the tercentenary royal visit. The barge flies the royal standard only when the Queen is on board.
OVERLEAF Pipe Major Bruce Hitchings of the Queen's Own Highlanders piping the Queen's return to HMY *Britannia*.

the timetable with them and check them constantly. The Queen has had forty years' practice in politely ending conversations, usually by taking half a step backwards and giving a broad smile. There will probably be no more than thirty or forty formal introductions with handshakes during the day (etiquette prescribes that the Queen shakes your hand; you do not squeeze hers), but several group conversations. The Palace will suggest that the groups are people doing similar work rather than mixed: a group of pupils, a group of staff, a group of governors, so that all of them will be able to join in all the conversation and no one will feel left out. They are encouraged to speak to her rather than wait until they are addressed.

The local press will be there, but only very rarely will there be any coverage in the national newspapers: royal visits are not primarily designed as publicity events. Only the unexpected would make the news, and the unexpected is what everyone is taking enormous trouble to avoid. Of course it can happen. When the Queen was caught in a snow storm in the Cotswolds, the astonished proprietor of a pub called the Cross Hands was asked if he could discreetly make a private room available for his sovereign. She had tea and then dinner there before the road was clear enough to drive back to Windsor.

The awayday visits differ from the honours system not just in their lower public profile but also because they are a mark of recognition for institutions rather than individuals. Their purpose is to demonstrate that the work of the institution and its staff matters not only to their customers, the public, their staff and the region, but also to the country. It is an affirmation of their place in the life of the nation – you may not feel your school or residential home or manufacturing company is all that important, but if it is important enough for the Queen to visit, then you are likely to look on it with a little extra pride. Someone is telling you that what you do in your ordinary working life matters, not just to you and your employer, but to Britain. The visit is another of the small threads which attaches the business of the nation to the apparatus of state. Most of an organization's contacts with the central

The Queen and the Duke of Edinburgh in Penrith, Cumbria, in May 1991. Every yard of the route is planned, timed and security checked before the visit. When the Queen is given more bouquets than she can carry, she passes them on to a Lady-in-Waiting.

government are tedious: tax returns, safety regulations, health inspections and all the apparatus of bureaucratic restriction and coercion. A royal visit shows that there is also a positive side to the relationship.

But could it not all be done through the post? The answer is that a great deal of the Queen's support of organizations is achieved without a visit. Her Private Secretaries are kept busy with endless requests for some form of royal recognition, and they also keep massive records of institutions, events and anniversaries the Queen will want to recognize in some way. One means is to accept the role of patron or president. About 3,000 organizations list a member of the Royal Family as patron under some title or other, and the Queen personally holds about 750 titles of patronage. She also accepts dedications and allows the use of her name or title, as in the Queen Elizabeth Hall or the Royal National Theatre. (There are eight and a half columns of organizations starting with 'Royal' in the London telephone directory.) She may send presents, messages, letters or telemessages of congratulation. The applications, the selection process and the final consent (or refusal) go on all the time without any personal contact. But still the Queen continues round her realm on royal visits, doing more leg-work than any but the most diligent journalists, as she has done for the past forty years. Forty years of planting trees, laying wreaths, cutting ribbons, dedicating churches, unveiling plaques, launching ships, laying foundation stones, accepting posies, signing visitors' books, shaking hands, drinking tea, eating lunch, inspecting guards of honour, walking round exhibitions and then taking the train, the plane or the car back to Buckingham Palace or Windsor or Sandringham or Balmoral.

One of the principal effects of a royal visit is to make the state seem more human and personal. Nation, state, country, government – these are all abstractions. Letters, certificates, warrants and messages of congratulation may all have been composed and sent out by secretaries. A real person, visible and touchable, travelling to your town or city and standing there in your hospital, laboratory or college is something different. It is an event. Very obviously a lot of people have taken immense trouble to make it happen. The Queen has bothered to come all this way specially. After it you feel more loyal, more patriotic, more a part of your country than you did before – 'a citizen of no mean city'. It also helps the Queen to know her country and her people. No one, and certainly not the Queen, is under any illusion that what she sees is a typical day in the normal life of the places she visits. Everyone is on their best behaviour and everything has been painted and polished for the occasion. Even so, forty years of travelling round Great Britain week after week builds up a picture and exposes changes which few people see in such detail over such a long period, and the tours of buildings, the inspecting of exhibitions, the briefings and the conversations give the Queen a unique informed insight into what the British people do with their working lives.

A look at the institutions which have received royal visits over the past 100 years would show much that is unchanged. Armed service units have always been prominent; so have churches and hospitals, municipal centres, large civil engineering projects and agricultural shows. There has, however, been one major change in emphasis since the war and especially during the Queen's reign, and one which shows how the Royal Family can use its influence positively without causing political problems: that change has been in the royal attitude to industry.

Before the Second World War there was a certain stigma about making money and especially making it through manufacturing, buying and selling goods. There was nothing wrong with *having* money; indeed the attitude seemed to be that you ought to have it, but, if you hadn't, you ought not to try and get it. It ought to come from the ownership of land, though the professions were acceptable. Trading for profit, however, came very low on the list of socially acceptable activities. The Royal Family did in fact have one mark of royal recognition exclusively for tradespeople: the Royal Warrant, which entitled approved suppliers of goods and services to members of the royal household to display the royal coat of arms (discreetly) on their premises, vehicles, goods and stationery. This still survives and is much sought after. The Queen, the Queen Mother, the Duke of Edinburgh and the Prince of Wales all grant warrants, and there are approximately 1,000 holders of warrants from one or more of them, 600 of them from the Queen. Four different departments in the Palace sit in judgement on warrant applications: the Privy Purse for private royal residences and the Queen's 'private expenditure as sovereign'; the Master of the Household's department for domestic needs – bedding, marmalade, chimney-sweeping; the Lord Chamberlain's office for bookbinders, calligraphers, computers and the crown jewellers; and the Royal Mews for horses, carriages and cars. (The

The Queen planting a prunus in front of Canongate Kirk,
Edinburgh, in June 1952, on her first visit to the Scottish capital
since her accession. With her is the Rev. R. Selby Wright.
OPPOSITE ABOVE The same tree in 1991, the fortieth year of
her reign.
BELOW Also in the fortieth year the same cleric, now Minister
Emeritus of Canongate Kirk, prepares for a service attended by the
Queen and Prince Philip on 30 June 1991.

Choosing new furnishing fabrics for the Palace of Holyroodhouse,
Edinburgh. Buckingham Palace, Windsor Castle and
Holyroodhouse are official residences of the sovereign. Sandringham
and Balmoral are the Queen's private property.

facts of the division of responsibilities are easier to explain than the logic.) If you study the list of royal warrant-holders, you will find kilt-makers, piano tuners, cartridge makers, ticket agents, handbag suppliers, dog food suppliers, toy makers, booksellers and manufacturers of woven name tapes. What you will not find in the list are any doctors, surgeons, solicitors, architects, stockbrokers, barristers or accountants; they are not in 'trade'.

A royal warrant was and is a form of recognition, but available to only a limited type of business; no one supplies offshore oil platforms for the personal use of members of the Royal Family. It is impossible to say when the importance of industry to Britain's survival dawned on the country's leadership; what is clear is that it had been realized by the Palace much earlier. The Duke of Edinburgh has a freedom to be controversial (though not party political) which is denied to the sovereign, and he was speaking out almost unfashionably and highly critically in the 1950s about Britain's export failures, lack of design and marketing skills, and declining industrial competitiveness. The Queen could only refer to them in the most impenetrable civil service code; but she could make statements by visits. As a result, the tours have for almost all her reign contained far more visits to factories, mines, offices, stores, shopping precincts and shipyards than her father or grandfather undertook. She also instituted, in 1966, a sort of industrial honours list, the Queen's Awards for Export and Technology. About 100 companies a year receive it under one of two headings, export achievement or technological innovation. Winners can fly a special flag and reproduce (discreetly) the insignia of the award on their packaging and stationery. Applicants have to fill up a long, complicated application form, and the Department of Trade and Industry has to check very carefully not only that the claims are true but also that the selected winners are not defrauding the Inland Revenue, artificially inflating their share price, polluting the environment or about to make an arrangement with their creditors.

7

THE FAMILY FIRM

Thursday 6 June was the seventieth anniversary of the British Federation of Festivals for Music, Dance and Speech. The Queen and the Duke of Edinburgh attended a reception for them at St James's Palace. The Federation is, of course, non-political, non-commercial, uncontroversial, their activities are praiseworthy and the anniversary was a suitably significant occasion. The Queen had also received the new South African ambassador, who presented his credentials, and had given audiences to the Deputy Commissioner of Police, the Permanent Secretary to the Lord Chancellor's Department, and the retiring head of Garrard's, the Crown jewellers. The Duke had come on from a lunch organized by the National Playing Fields Association, of which he is president.

ABOVE The Royal Military Academy receives a royal visit. The Queen went to Sandhurst in April 1991 to present new colours to mark 250 years of officer training in the British Army.
OPPOSITE Prince Philip in Dover visiting the Association of Dunkirk Little Ships Fleet on the fiftieth anniversary of the evacuation. The Royal Family has strong naval ties: King George VI fought at Jutland, Prince Philip fought in the Second World War and the Duke of York fought in the Falklands.

The Princess of Wales visiting Marlow on 6 June 1991. On her way
back to London she visited Prince William, who was in hospital
recovering from a depressed fracture of the skull after an accident
with a golf club at school.
OPPOSITE The Prince of Wales attends the Golden Jubilee of the
Parachute Regiment in June 1990. There is a special affinity
between the Royal Family and the armed services: many retired
officers hold high positions in the court.

On the same day the Prince of Wales was presenting prizes on behalf of
the Prince's Youth Business Trust, of which he is president.

The Princess of Wales was in Buckinghamshire visiting the Royal
Grammar School at High Wycombe and the Marlow Community Hospital.
On her way back to an evening gala organ recital at St Martin's-in-the-
Fields in London, she stopped off in Denham to visit the Martin-Baker
Aircraft company. She also visited her eldest son, Prince William, who was

in hospital recovering from a depressed skull fracture as a result of an accident with a golf club.

Meanwhile the Duke of York, was presenting photographic awards for the Hearing Research Trust, of which is he patron.

The British Knitting and Clothing Export Council was holding its annual general meeting at London's Berkeley Hotel. Princess Anne, The Princess Royal, attended as president. After the lunch she flew to Northumberland

The Duke of York, and Prince Edward, with the Prince of Wales in the background, at a reception during the state visit of President Mubarak of Egypt in July 1991. When the Queen came to the throne there were only three other direct members of the family to support her in public engagements. Today there are nine.

OPPOSITE June 1990: the Princess Royal visits HMS *Collingwood*. In 1990 she undertook 768 public engagements, more than any other member of the Royal Family.

Princess Margaret talking to guests at a reception in Windsor Castle.
Between them the Royal Family, including the Kents and the
Gloucesters, attend some 3,000 public engagements a year in the
UK and another 1,000 overseas.
OPPOSITE The Queen and Princess Alexandra. The list of
organizations which have a member of the Royal Family as a patron
is 170 pages long.
OVERLEAF Derby Day 1991, the Queen and the Queen Mother
watching the race before the Derby in which the Queen's horse
came fourth.

and visited the Save the Children Fund shop in Hexham before opening a
new golf club and conference centre near by.

That same evening Princess Margaret went to a preview of the Antiques
Fair at Olympia in aid of the National Society for the Prevention of Cruelty
to Children, of which she is president.

The 6th of June was not an unusual day, but it provides a good illustration
of one of the biggest changes in the character of the monarchy during the
forty years of the Queen's reign: it has grown into a family business. When
the Queen came to the throne, there were only three 'working' members of
the direct Royal Family to support her: the Duke of Edinburgh, the Queen

The Queen Mother in the royal suite inside Epsom grandstand for the Derby. In 1990, the year of her ninetieth birthday, she carried out 122 public engagements.

Mother and Princess Margaret. Today there are nine – the original three plus her four children and two daughters-in-law – and she already has six grandchildren. The nuclear family of 1952 had turned into something like a dynasty by 1992.

There is no constitutional role for any member of the Royal Family except the Queen; they belong to the 'nation' and not the 'state' side of the job. The children and grandchildren and Princess Margaret are nevertheless in the direct line of succession. They 'belong' to the apparatus of the state and are seen as part of it. As with the Queen, if the nation identifies with them, it subconsciously endorses the British legal and political system of which the Queen is head. They may not appoint prime ministers or dissolve parliaments, but by the visits they pay, the functions they attend, the roles they accept and the activities they support, they play their part in stitching the working and social life of the nation into the fabric of the state. Over the years they have not so much eased the burdens on the Queen as increased the range of royal influence. Between them the 'direct' Royal Family together with the Kents and Gloucesters personally attend something like 3,000 UK functions in any given year, and another 1,000 overseas. There have to be regular meetings at which all their secretaries get together to sort out their programmes for the coming months, not only to see that engagements do not clash but also to check whether the family is giving too much or too little time to a particular form of activity or part of the country. There are also frequent informal contacts.

The Queen has by far the largest list of organizations of which she is the patron, but her patronage is different in kind from all the others. She never takes an active part in the work of the organization. The rest of the family are not so restricted and usually have several organizations in which they are seriously interested – the Princess Royal with Save the Children, the Prince of Wales with various youth and business organizations, the Duke of Edinburgh with wildlife, sport and industry. The growing size of the family has inevitably brought a much greater spread of interests, enabling a far larger number of interest groups to feel they have some royal recognition – quite literally a friend at court. It works with other groupings as well – not just dancing or sport or photography, but social groupings: mothers of young children may not live the lives of the Princess of Wales or the Duchess of York, but they believe they share the same maternal feelings and anxieties, just as the elderly feel they have lived through the same experiences as the Queen Mother and believe she shares beliefs and standards that they see dying out around them.

The members of the Royal Family do something else as well, beyond extending the range and variety of royal patronage. They can act as scouts, carrying out a form of royal reconnaissance to see if 'territory' is 'safe' for the Queen. Would it, for example, offend an important number of people if the Queen were to patronize a charity devoted to AIDS sufferers? It was not necessary for the Queen herself to test the water; the Princess of Wales was filmed in an AIDS hospice holding hands with a patient, and the generally approving response showed that there would be no public outcry. And although the job of the monarchy is on the whole to respond to change rather than start it, it was possible for the Prince of Wales to use the influence of

OVERLEAF The Queen having her portrait painted in Buckingham Palace by Andrew Festing in March 1991.

Rubens's painting of *The Holy Family with St Francis* (*foreground*) and Domenichino's *St Agnes* being restored in Friary Court, Buckingham Palace. The Royal Collection is one of Britain's major art treasure houses and a part is on permanent public exhibition in the Queen's Gallery, Buckingham Palace.

the Royal Family without involving the Queen when he took the initiative in giving respectability to less conventional forms of medicine not recognized by the medical establishment. In that case the response, even though generally favourable, did suggest that the time was perhaps not quite ripe for the Queen to accept a presidency of an institute for holistic medicine.

The number of organizations supported by members of the Royal Family may be large, but they can be grouped under quite a small number of headings: charities, health, sport, industry, arts, sciences, environment, education, welfare services and religion. There is, though, one other area, perhaps more widely patronized than any of the others, and one which has always been especially close to the British Royal Family, as indeed it is to governments everywhere: the armed services.

On 15 June 1991 at precisely 11 a.m. the Queen arrived in an open carriage at Horse Guards Parade to a forty-one-gun salute from the Royal Horse Artillery in Hyde Park for the annual ceremony of Trooping the Colour. 1,500 men and 200 horses put on an eighty-minute military display for her and her family and for 7,000 members of the public who were lucky enough to obtain places – about 100,000 applied. It is Britain's biggest military parade of the year and dates back to the days when soldiers in battle only knew where they were by the position of the regiment's flag. If they did not know what it looked like, they were in real trouble, so it was 'trooped' in front of them before the battle to make sure they would recognize it when the fight was on. Colours have not in fact been carried into battle since the Crimean War, 1854–6, so the practical value of the ceremony is limited. Its popularity, however, is beyond question, and it is another reminder of the close links between the sovereign and the military.

The history of most of the world's older states is dominated by wars, and its military leaders are the national heroes of fact and legend. This is hardly surprising; for most of recorded history it has been wars that have created the identity and secured the survival of states and nations. A country like England with 1,000 years of history as a single independent nation is likely to have more military heroes, traditions, ceremonies, buildings and memorials than most. Obviously the Royal Family is and always has been closely bound up with the country's wars and the men and women who fought them. Many early monarchs were themselves military commanders – William the Conqueror and Richard the Lionheart, Edward I and Henvy V – and almost all of them took an active and direct interest in the strategy and tactics of warfare on land and sea. No British monarch has actually commanded the army in battle since George II at Dettingen in 1743, but the connection has remained strong. The Queen's father, husband and two of her sons were professional serving sailors. George VI fought in the Battle of Jutland, Prince Philip fought in the Second World War, the Duke of York fought in the

Falklands. It is a very direct connection; recruits take The Queen's Shilling, new officers accept The Queen's Commission, they serve on Her Majesty's ships or in royal regiments, or regiments with royal names, or of which the Queen or members of the Royal Family are colonels-in-chief, and the highest gallantry awards are named after her father and her great-great-grandmother. The Royal Family between them number several hundred service organizations in their patronage; in the 170-page list of institutions with which they are identified, there are fifty entries under 'Naval' and 'Navy' alone.

Trooping the Colour is one of the most popular events of London's summer season. About 100,000 people apply for the places for the eighty-minute display; there is room for only 7,000.

OPPOSITE The royal party returns from Horse Guards Parade to Buckingham Palace at the end of the ceremony of Trooping the Colour. This is the view of the Victoria Memorial and the Mall which the Queen sees from her balcony.

OVERLEAF The Queen visits the 5th Airborne Division on Salisbury Plain. Hundreds of service organizations figure on the patronage list of members of the Royal Family.

For the past 100 years or so the Royal Family have been especially at ease with service people, and service people have been especially at ease with them. If you look behind the ancient titles of senior courtiers you find an abundance of service ranks: in 1991–2 Black Rod was an Air Chief Marshal and his deputy was an Air Commodore, the Master of the Household was a Rear-Admiral and his deputy was a Lieutenant-Colonel, the Comptroller of the Lord Chamberlain's office and his assistant were also Lieutenant-Colonels, and so was the Crown Equerry, the Keeper of the Privy Purse was a Major, and the Marshal of the Diplomatic Corps was a Lieutenant-General. Senior officers are, after all, loyal, security dependable, politically impartial, dutiful, disciplined, experienced organizers and comfortable in hierarchies, though there is no doubt that they give the court a different tone from what you would find if it were staffed by accountants, actors or advertising executives. In a way this identification with the armed services needs no explanation; as Head of State the Queen is head of the armed services, and the defence of the realm is one of the two essential duties of any state. It is also the less controversial of the two; keeping order within the realm can tremble on the brink of party politics, as it did during the 1984 miners' strike and the London anti-poll tax rally in March 1990, and has done at various political demonstrations over the years. Fighting for your country against its enemies is an expression of unity rather than a response to division and dissent.

It is not, however, in the Queen's role as Head of State that the real importance of the military connection lies. Of course it matters very much constitutionally that the services should be as it were parallel with the government and both answerable to the Crown, rather than totally under the control of the government of the day, but discharging the duties of that role does not actively occupy much of the Queen's time. No one expected her to be poring over maps in the Arabian desert discussing tank movements with General Schwarzkopf. The continuing importance of the relationship between the sovereign and the armed forces does not come from her official position – it comes from their personal loyalty to the Queen and the Royal Family.

Obviously we do not feel patriotic simply because we have a Royal Family. People fight and die for their nation whether it is a republic, a military dictatorship, a constitutional monarchy or a rebel faction within a state to

On arrival at the Palace of Holyroodhouse the Queen is given the
keys to the city of Edinburgh and inspects the guard.

which they feel no personal or collective allegiance. In the Second World
War the Americans were fighting under an elected president, the Germans
under a military dictator, the Japanese under a god-emperor, the Russians
under a totalitarian party boss and the British under a constitutional
monarch. No one could point to one or other of those nations and say they
fought with greater or less courage and endurance because of the form of
government under which they served.

Certainly the British armed forces feel a strong loyalty to the Queen and the Royal Family. At the higher levels this is for much the same reason as the Foreign and Commonwealth Office's close identification with the sovereign: to show their absolute loyalty to their country while distancing themselves from politicians, for whom as a breed the armed services have even less respect than diplomats have. For the broad mass of servicemen this distancing is not such a powerful motive, but it has to be remembered that something like half of them will have voted against whatever government is in power; even if it is a coalition, they will have voted against half its members. For most serving soldiers the Queen and the Royal Family form a compelling focus of allegiance and a powerful symbol to represent their own families, who provide the strongest single motive for risking their lives in battle. Many serving soldiers wrote to the Queen during the Gulf War to express their personal loyalty and pride, and it is clear from those letters that they were not spurred on by an emotional commitment to the government's Middle Eastern policy. They were fighting for Queen and country.

It is impossible to measure if a hereditary monarchy like Britain's is any more powerful than other forms of government in encouraging patriotism. There may well be an advantage, though, in the non-political nature of the monarchy, especially in a war that is not for national survival. The United States Army in Vietnam suffered a moral debacle; the war was the subject of deep and passionate political division at home and their President, as head of state and head of the armed services, was deeply committed to one side of the argument. Would morale have gone so badly to pieces if the head of state had been above and outside the political battle? And the same question can be asked about the national trauma after the war had ended: it was hard for the state to honour the returning veterans too enthusiastically when politicians were all trying to distance themselves from the whole messy business. When the head of state is an elected politician and his advisers tell him that there are a great many votes to be lost by identifying himself in any way with the war, there is no one above him to honour the returning troops or lead the nation in remembrance of the dead no matter how much people may still be disputing the justice of the cause for which they died.

A monarchy provides a non-partisan focus for allegiance, and a hereditary monarchy provides a permanent one. This may or may not be an advantage over other forms of government in motivating the armed forces in war, but it serves another function. If the services are loyal to the sovereign, they are by implication loyal to the state and the government. There is no universal law which says that armies (and navies and air forces) will always be loyal to governments. In newly independent countries they are often the effective government and, even when they are not, they are very often the force that makes or breaks the government. They are always the greatest physical power in the land, and frequently more trusted and admired than politicians. Even in more mature democracies the army can become deeply disaffected from the government of the day and, especially if it is weak and unpopular, the government can find it difficult to make the generals do what it wants. More often it compromises, allowing the army to develop as a semi-autonomous power within the state, self-regulating and almost outside the control of the elected politicians. It became clear during the Balkan crisis in July 1991 that this had happened in Yugoslavia.

It is hard for politicians to win the trust, respect and loyalty of soldiers. It is nothing like so hard for monarchs. It is over 300 years since a sizeable section of the British army withdrew its support from the Crown and the government to replace James II by William of Orange, and nobody wants it to happen again. Clearly there is no immediate danger of it, but the strongest safeguard is the personal and collective loyalty that the armed services feel towards the sovereign. They are *her* forces, not the government's, but the government is still *her* government acting in her name and with her authority. The armed forces cannot defy the government without betraying the sovereign's trust.

And so, year after year, the Queen and the rest of the Royal Family take salutes, inspect guards of honour, attend tattoos, present colours, bestow honours, award medals, launch ships, lay wreaths, visit aerodromes and observe manœuvres all round the United Kingdom and in any other countries where Her Majesty's forces are stationed. No one expects all this to increase the admirals' or generals' admiration for politicians or their respect for cabinet decisions or directives from the Ministry of Defence, but it does mean they know that in the end they have no alternative but to accept them.

8

MEETING
THE PEOPLE

On Tuesday 18 June the Queen received 256 letters. In fact she received a great many more official ones, but these were letters from members of the public. There was nothing unusual about that day; the average is between 200 and 300 a day every day or some 60,000 a year. (At one stage in Silver Jubilee Year it was running at around 4,000 a day.) In the course of a forty-year reign that adds up to something approaching $2\frac{1}{2}$ million letters.

All the letters were, as usual, taken straight into the Queen's office unopened. She looked through them and selected about a dozen to read for herself; according to her staff, over the years she has developed a sixth sense for which are likely to be unusual. Where relevant, she wrote a brief note on the letter to guide her staff as to the reply she wanted to make. The letters were then taken away for the staff to answer.

Not surprisingly the letters cover a tremendous range of topics. Some are good wishes, some want advice on where to buy a Welsh corgi, some are

ABOVE The Queen talks to children in Surrey in April 1991. She started royal walkabouts in 1970. They are very popular with the crowds, but a nightmare for the security service.

hardship cases that the welfare services cannot help, some are abusive, some are requests for money, some are clearly part of an organized lobbying campaign, some are from people who are, to put it mildly, extremely eccentric. Some are straightforward and factual, and can be answered by the five full-time staff in the Information and Correspondence Office. For practical purposes, however, most letters fall into one of two main categories: one is what you might call 'fan mail' and the other is 'cries for help'. The 'fan mail' – personal greetings, criticism, letters from children – are answered by her Ladies-in-Waiting on the Queen's behalf; over the years they have refined the art of being non-committal without sounding distant or impersonal. 'Cries for help' often begin along the lines 'I am writing to you because I do not know where else to turn.' These are usually dealt with by the private secretaries. Quite often they can help by pointing the correspondent in the right direction. Sometimes they can do little more than pass the letter to the appropriate government department. There is no evidence that people are treated differently because they choose to write to the Queen instead of direct to, say, the Department of Social Security; on the other hand it is a fair guess that, if a letter arrives in a government office from Buckingham Palace, it is less likely to get lost or be ignored.

At first sight the Queen's level of personal interest in her mail from the general public may seem surprising. It would not be unreasonable for her to leave it all to her staff and let them select any special letters they think she would like to see. It would not be unreasonable for them to answer her letters themselves and say something like, ' … I acknowledge your letter to Her Majesty. The question, however, falls under the responsibility of the Department of Health, and I have accordingly forwarded your letter to them.' Her more personal response is closer to what you might expect from an MP to a constituent, rather than from a sovereign to a subject. In the same way you might expect an MP to send a telemessage of birthday congratulations to

OVERLEAF The Queen in the Audience Room in Buckingham Palace, reading her correspondence from the general public. She receives between 200 and 300 letters per day. It went up to 4,000 a day in her Silver Jubilee year. Letters are sent up unopened; she always selects a sample to open and read personally.

centenarians in his constituency, whereas in fact every centenarian receives a birthday telemessage from the Queen, and another on their 105th birthday and every year thereafter. In the early 1950s she sent about 200 centenary birthday telegrams and 10 for 105th or higher birthdays; in 1990 the number had risen to 2,227 for centenarians and 262 for the 105s and upwards. She also sends congratulations to diamond wedding couples – 1,194 in 1955, 6,129 in 1990. If you include messages to people overseas and Commonwealth subjects, the Queen's annual total in 1990 was 13,537. It appears to be democratic rather than monarchical behaviour.

Obviously nothing could be less democratic than a hereditary monarchy, either in the formal sense that monarchs do not offer themselves for re-election or in the colloquial sense of living in a suburban semi and catching the bus to work. And yet in a democratic country with a sovereign parliament the monarchy – the whole system, not just the present Queen – depends for its survival on popular consent. If large majorities in both Houses of Parliament voted for its abolition, then – assuming the government had a mandate for abolition – there is no constitutional provision for retaining it. Certainly, if a large majority of the voters really wanted to get rid of the monarchy, there would be no shortage of politicians anxious to pick up their votes by writing abolition into their election manifesto. As Prince Philip said to the Canadians, 'The answer to this question of the monarchy is very simple – if people don't like it, they should change it. . . . The monarchy exists not for its own benefit, but for that of the country.'

There is, though, a particular problem about being a monarch in a democracy: how do you actually meet 'real' people? It is all too easy to spend a busy year meeting hordes of officials and representatives, generals and admirals, peers and cabinet ministers, presidents and chairmen, mayors and councillors, executive directors and top civil servants, and never come into contact with people whom you meet simply as themselves rather than as representatives or servants of an institution or an interest group. This problem is not exclusive to royalty; it confronts top people in all large institutions. Lord Marks was so concerned by the danger of remoteness that he insisted all directors and head office executives spend one day each week in a Marks & Spencer store in order to stay in touch with the realities of the business. Many cabinet ministers have found that their weekly constituency 'surgery' is at least as much and probably more use to them than to the constituents

A garden party in progress at Buckingham Palace. The names of
guests are put forward by various 'sponsoring organizations', but
individuals are invited personally by the Lord Chamberlain
on the Queen's behalf.
OVERLEAF The Buckingham Palace garden being made ready for
a royal garden party. The thirty-nine-acre garden has the largest
camomile lawn in Britain.

Holyroodhouse garden party: guests talk to Princess Alice,
Duchess of Gloucester, seated on the left. Princess Alice is in her
ninetieth year.
OPPOSITE ABOVE The High Constables at the Palace of
Holyroodhouse dressed for duty at the garden party in July 1991.
BELOW The band of the Gordon Highlanders play a little light
music for the entertainment of guests at Holyroodhouse.

society no longer carries much weight in the political nation. Its last official event was abolished in 1957, when the Queen ended the practice of having debutantes presented to her at court; the event was replaced by the third garden party and she radically changed the nature of the occasion by inviting a much broader cross-section of guests. Even so, the garden parties on their own do not produce a representative sample of her subjects. Most of the guests chosen by the sponsors play some form of role in public life within their community. So in 1970 the Queen and the Duke of Edinburgh brought in another innovation; it was not publicized in advance like the abolition of debutantes, but it has become a permanent fixture even if it is a highly movable feast: the royal walkabout.

On the afternoon of 15 May in Drake Place, Washington DC the Queen was hugged by Alice Frazier, a fifteen-stone great-grandmother. In any of her predecessors' reigns this would have been impossible, as it would have been for the early part of her own. Sovereigns never walked about in public. They were remote and protected, just glimpsed behind the windows of cars and carriages. It was more like displaying an icon than a visit from a human being, a sober and sombre version of the parading of statues of saints through Mediterranean towns on church festivals. The Royal Family made the change because they felt the old style of remote unapproachability was out of tune with the popular mood that had developed in the 1960s. Even if people did not actively resent it, there was often disappointment at having waited so long for so little. It may seem a small and unimportant change now, but it signalled a major shift in royal attitudes, acting to bring the monarchy to the people. There were strong security arguments against it (it is always something of a security hazard), but the Queen and her advisers felt very keenly that it was what people wanted from a royal visit. The first walkabout took place in New Zealand in 1970 – despite the fact that 'walkabout' is an Australian Aboriginal term – and, although there have been occasional alerts and alarms, it has become over the years one of the most popular parts of royal visits and the regular practice of the Queen and all the Royal Family.

The walkabouts reflect the importance the Palace attaches to the Queen's being head of the whole nation; to be the monarch of the middle class would be as damaging as to be the monarch of the metropolis. For the same reason, when she visits organizations on her awaydays, the Queen and the whole

Royal walkabouts are unpredictable. On a visit to a housing
project in Washington DC during her visit to the USA the Queen
was suddenly hugged by Alice Frazier, a fifteen-stone
great-grandmother.

Royal Family always meet privates as well as generals, nurses as well as
consultants, and foremen as well as chairmen. Others may divide the nation
into sections and factions – left and right, upper and lower, labour and
management, black and white, Catholic and Protestant, urban and rural,
North and South – but the sovereign has to see and treat the whole nation
as a single unit. During the General Strike of 1926 King George V had to be

As Princess Elizabeth the Queen served with the ATS during the
Second World War and learnt to strip and service an engine. 'We
had sparking plugs last night all through dinner,' the Queen (now
the Queen Mother) told a friend.

(and was) on the side of order against disorder, but he did not have to be (and was not) on the side of the coal owners against the mineworkers. In this he differed from the general British establishment attitude. In the same way Edward VIII as Prince of Wales visited an unemployment black spot in South Wales and was overheard indiscreetly muttering that something had to be done about it. As a result, many establishment figures were very upset and a lot of miners' families warmed to the Royal Family in a way they did not warm to the government.

Perhaps the most important and convincing demonstration of this determination to be monarch of all the people occurred during the London blitz. King George VI could have chosen or been persuaded to spend the Second World War in one of his colonies or dominions; there were strong arguments in favour of this. Certainly the Royal Family could have decided to move its base to Windsor, or Holyrood for that matter, for the duration of the war. Instead they chose to stay in London and share the blitz with their subjects. They went round the bombed streets in the aftermath of the raids, talked to Londoners in the rubble of their former homes, toured stricken provincial cities, visited the injured in hospital, had tea with firemen, air-raid wardens and voluntary workers, and created a bond with the nation which still survives. Britain's older citizens, say sixty and over, feel for the Queen Mother an emotion which goes far beyond the normal respect and loyalty of a subject for a sovereign. In the same way the image of the young Princess Elizabeth in Army Transport Service uniform taking a course in the repair and maintenance of three-ton army trucks creates a fellow-feeling for her generation to set in the scale against the not inconsiderable difference in income and lifestyle which separates them.

If one of the aims of the monarchy is to secure the personal respect and loyalty of the people, the evidence suggests that it has been successful. Almost all opinion polls show a massive level of support and approval. The Queen herself usually scores something like 80% or 90%. In a more detailed MORI poll early in 1990, 63% of the respondents said they thought Britain would be worse off if the monarchy was abolished and only 6% thought it would be better off. They also thought it would be less united (53% to 5%) and, rather surprisingly, less democratic (37% to 10%). (Perhaps it is fair to add that 26% of the sample were under the illusion that the Queen was head of the Bank of England.) In another survey eighteen months earlier by SCPR, respondents in Britain and West Germany were asked about their sources of national pride. For the West Germans their constitution was the first choice (30%) with economic achievements second at 17%; 51% chose the constitution as one of their sources of pride. In Britain the monarchy came first with 37% and scientific achievements second at 22%; 65% chose the monarchy as one of their sources of national pride. For some of the respondents the choice may have been little more than a lukewarm preference, but for others it is clearly more profound. In a survey of 1,000 people, between 200 and 300 supplied reports of royal dreams to the author of *Dreams About Her Majesty*. Allowing for those who had had royal dreams but forgotten them, the author conjectured that about a third of the population dream about the Queen or her family. The dreamers included republicans and militant Communists, but the Queen always appeared pleasant and charming, and usually in non-royal settings – in an Earl's Court bedsit, a Yorkshire farm and a caravan, and as a table tennis player, a lift operator, a lorry driver and a goalkeeper. Nearly 50% of the dreams involved having tea.

Is there a reason for all this? In his book *The English Constitution*, written 125 years ago, Walter Bagehot said that the best reason why monarchy was a strong form of government was that it was an intelligible government. He went on to say, of the wedding of the future Edward VII: 'A family on the throne is an interesting idea also. It brings down the pride of sovereignty to the level of petty life.... The women – one half of the human race at least – care fifty times more for a marriage than a ministry ... so long as the human heart is strong and the human reason weak, royalty will be strong because it appeals to diffused feeling, and Republics weak because they appeal to understanding.' If Bagehot's remark about women seems sexist and dated, it should be recorded that in the 1988 survey of sources of national pride the Royal Family was named first by 29% of men and 46% of women.

There is certainly a sense in which, although only a few people belong to the Royal Family, the Royal Family belongs to everyone. Commentators sometimes refer disparagingly to 'Britain's royal soap opera'. Perhaps they do not understand the power and importance of programmes like *Coronation*

Office workers in Penrith waiting for a glimpse of the Queen during her visit to Cumbria in May 1991. The route is checked in advance by the local police and the Palace security staff.

Street and *Eastenders*. In a time when fewer and fewer people live in neighbourly communities these programmes provide an important substitute for village gossip. One of the principal social functions of gossip, over and above the simple exchange of information, is to help a community form, share and update its moral standards: 'She shouldn't have done that, should she?' or 'I think it was his fault as much as hers.' A century ago the subject of the conversation would have been the family down the street or across the village green. Today we make do with the customers of the Queen Vic and the Rover's Return.

But there is one real family which is never out of the papers or off the screen. Whether the national obsession with them is healthy or unhealthy is an academic question: every newspaper editor knows that the slightest hint of a rift or row within the Royal Family will sell more copies. Like the other, fictional families, they serve as a moral touchstone; their behaviour is a starting point for discussions about how much time husbands should spend away from their wives, or whether mothers should leave their small children behind when they go on holiday, or whether a married couple with children should stay together or face reality and separate. The fact that their wealth and lifestyle sets them apart does not stop them being examples of behaviour and standards, or excuse them from moral judgements, any more than it does the characters of *Dallas* or *Dynasty*. There is a difference, nevertheless: the audience has no involvement other than dramatic interest in the behaviour of the fictional characters in television serials. No one is proud of JR or Alexis; but the Queen is 'our Queen', and it is clear from the opinion polls that people feel proud of her.

The feeling of pride in someone has a strong element of possession in it. People are proud of their own children because their identity, their ego, is bound up with them; they are not proud of strangers' children, however praiseworthy. They are proud of their national sporting heroes, but not of the sporting heroes of other countries, no matter how admirable. Very few people feel pride in the government in the same way that they feel it in the Royal Family. We approve or disapprove of governments because of the sort of things they do; we approve or disapprove of the Royal Family because of the sort of people they are. This means that if the Royal Family behave in a way that we think is wrong, it can be truly upsetting for those who identify with them and feel pride in them.

The Queen talking to guests at a garden party at Hillsborough
Castle in Northern Ireland in June 1991.

Part of the Americans' trauma over the Watergate scandal was that it
concerned not the sort of thing their head of government did but the sort of
person their President was: the head of state was caught up in a shabby and
shady conspiracy. Had it been a head of government's action, they would
have felt angry, but because it was their head of state they felt guilty. They
were implicated. In the same way and much more powerfully, because of

the permanence of a hereditary monarchy, the British people are not merely interested in the behaviour of the Royal Family – they are involved and implicated in it. We assume that their behaviour, their moral standards and their values will be the same as ours. When they conflict, we are not just irritated – we are anxious; and we are anxious not just because we think *they* are wrong but because we think *we* may be wrong. We have to check our standards out with our friends and neighbours, and with the writers in newspapers and magazines, and the callers on chat shows and the panellists on discussion programmes. We may end up deciding that perhaps we have failed to move with the times and there's probably no harm in couples living together before marriage, or we may decide that standards are standards and even the twenty-seventh in line to the throne should set an example. Either way we are demonstrating the importance of the Royal Family to our personal lives. We are also demonstrating to the Royal Family the importance of affirming values and setting standards which their subjects can identify with, and of ensuring that their private as well as their public actions are of the sort that the nation is happy to be implicated in and involved in: to behave, in fact, in a way that the country can be proud of.

If they succeed, they play a part in creating a cohesive and unified nation. There are many elements to national unity which do not depend on the words and deeds of a sovereign and a royal family: a shared language, a shared history, a shared culture, a single political system, a single legal system, a single financial system, a single administrative system, a single currency. Republics have all these just as much as monarchies. Another forceful instrument of unity is a single religion and a single moral system, which gives a powerful cohesive and regulatory force to Islamic states, and reinforces the authority of governments if they can harness it. If they cannot, as the Shah of Iran could not, the opposition can turn a political campaign into a religious crusade. If they can, as the Ayatollah Khomeini could, they can survive any number of reverses and disasters. Britain, like most western states, can no longer command a religious or moral unifying system on the Islamic model to reinforce the authority of government. Northern Ireland provides the clearest example of the dangers when some of the population do not share the values of the state in which they live and can harness the moral force of religion to their political opposition. There is also the visible danger in the inner cities that communities will develop which reject the moral standards of the rest of the nation and feel no sense of unity with or loyalty to the country they live in and the government they live under. National unity sounds like no more than a pompous platitude until you see it start to crumble as it did in the Soviet Union and in Yugoslavia in 1991.

It would be hard to argue that the forty years of the Queen's reign have seen an increase in the feeling of national unity; most people believe it has declined. It would be equally hard to get any general agreement on the chief reasons for the decline, though clearly there are several. The contrast is most obvious to those who remember the Second World War, when shared hardship and danger helped to create a sense of shared values and common purpose, which did not survive the growth of peace and prosperity, quite apart from all the other changes and pressures of the past forty years or so. There is no doubt, however, that one of the main functions of the sovereign as Head of the Nation is to act as a force for national unity. This is not something that can be achieved by pious exhortations; it is only possible when the broad mass of people accept the authority of the state, and obey its laws out of something more positive than fear of detection and punishment – out of conviction rather than out of fear of conviction. This implies a sense of belonging, of being a part of the nation and the state, of sharing its standards and values. Parliament can incorporate these in its laws, but the Queen and the Royal Family personalize them in a human and visible way: it is easier to identify with a person and a family than with institutions and regulations. As Head of the State and the Nation the Queen is uniquely placed to harness people's personal values to the state, the political system and the government, but only so long as people see her, know about her, know what she stands for (and will not stand for), identify with her, and believe that her behaviour, her standards and her values correspond with their own. So, while the Queen and the Royal Family could not be less democratic in any formal sense, they have to behave just as democratically as if they had to stand for re-election every five years like politicians and governments.

9

COPING WITH
THE MEDIA

Sunday 10 February 1991 was not a day of rest for the Buckingham Palace Press Secretary. The Gulf War had been in progress for three weeks, and the *Sunday Times* devoted its leader to criticisms of members of the Royal Family for continuing to play golf, take Caribbean holidays and go to parties at a time of national crisis.

There is nothing recent about press criticism of members of the Royal Family, but for some reason the *Sunday Times* leader had an electrifying effect on the rest of the national press. The phone calls began on the Saturday evening, before the article had actually appeared (the *Sunday Times* had faxed copies to journalists on other newspapers) and the Press Secretary had to deal with fifteen or twenty phone calls. On Sunday the telephone hardly stopped ringing – there were about fifty more phone calls to deal with.

The next morning and for most of the following week the Royal Family came under intense scrutiny in the national media. The original *Sunday Times*

ABOVE The Queen making a speech in Lisbon during a state visit
to Portugal in 1985. In her public appearances she has to be aware
of microphones as well as cameras.

The first broadcast, 13 October 1940. The fourteen-year-old Princess
Elizabeth, watched by Princess Margaret (aged ten), speaking to
the children of the Empire.
OVERLEAF The Queen reads the daily papers on the train to
Edinburgh in June 1991. Every morning she is sent a summary of
all press references to the Royal Family in the national media.

charge of not pulling their weight in the Gulf War was broadened and
deepened. The younger members were accused of a too frivolous and insen-
sitive lifestyle, of taking advantage of their privileged position, of not doing
enough for their Civil List allowances. The Queen was not personally cri-
ticized – even the original *Sunday Times* leader said that she had 'behaved
impeccably' – but there were renewed demands that she should pay tax on

been over for only seven years and the unifying effect of hardship and austerity carried through; it was still the world of doing your bit rather than doing your thing. Food rationing was still in force, and the spirit of rationing pervaded the Buckingham Palace Press Office: information was distributed sparingly. The media were welcome at selected public events, but were not expected to show any interest in the private lives of the Royal Family or to criticize their behaviour. They were given what was considered appropriate, and the rest of the press operation was purely response to enquiries – and usually a brief and uninformative response.

The change began in 1957. Malcolm Muggeridge wrote an article in the *Saturday Evening Post* entitled 'Does England Really Need a Queen?' criticizing the monarchy as snobbish, obsolete and disadvantageous. Today it would hardly raise an eyebrow, but in 1957 its effect was volcanic. There was public outrage. He received letters of obscene and violent abuse. Some contained human excrement. He was unofficially but comprehensively banned from the BBC. Nevertheless his article was published, as was a similar one by Lord Altrincham (John Grigg), also in 1957, in the *National and English Review* criticizing the remoteness of the Queen from her subjects and the unrepresentatively upper-class nature of her court. It was not a freak storm, but the herald of a change in the climate. The change came in the 1960s.

The Sixties were the low point for the monarchy in its relationship with the press and the broadcasters. It was the decade of novelty, change, populism, classlessness, individuality and licence. It was not a comfortable decade for an institution which was ancient, traditional, aristocratic, structured, conformist and respectable. As the decade wore on supporters of the institution began to wonder whether the old publicity policy of keeping the drawbridge up and the portcullis down was still in the best interests of the monarchy. Should the Royal Family's press advisers actively seek favourable publicity rather than simply try to fend off unfavourable publicity?

Two events in 1969 answered the question. A film unit was given unprecedented freedom to record a year in the life of the Royal Family for BBC and ITV, and the 110-minute film *Royal Family* was shown on 21 June. Ten days later the investiture of Prince Charles as Prince of Wales was staged as an outside broadcast for television in Caernarvon Castle. The two events were not only extremely popular with the television audience, they also seemed to release a flood of national goodwill towards the Queen and the

The press in waiting at Santa Barbara, California, during the 1983
royal visit to the USA. Some royal events may have as many as
1,000 accredited press representatives in attendance.

Royal Family that had been held back for nearly ten years. In terms of their
press and television image, the long winter of the 1960s ended in the summer
of 1969; but the success of positive publicity created a new problem which
has not yet been solved.

Clearly the policy of keeping the press at bay had failed, but the alternative
also had its dangers. If the Palace did seek publicity, how would they be any
different from the film stars, pop singers and all the other publicity seekers

An early lesson in media hardware: Prince Henry is shown the
secrets of film cameras by the BBC cameraman of the royal film
Elizabeth R while they wait in the quadrangle of Buckingham Palace
for the Queen to return from Trooping the Colour, 1991.

and media manipulators? How would they answer the charge of putting on
a show, of scripting a royal soap opera?

Publicity has always been an important weapon in the royal armoury.
Much of the benefit of a royal visit to an organization is the publicity it gives
them. Royal visits abroad help to publicize British tourism and British
exports. Royal patronage and their presence at lunches, dinners and gala
concerts publicize charities and increase public attendance and contri-
butions. The Christmas broadcast sends the Queen's image and message to
all the countries in the Commonwealth. The royal connection also helps to

publicize ideas and causes: the needs of young people in inner cities, holistic medicine, environmentally friendly agriculture, AIDS, world hunger. In all these ways the Royal Family are bestowing the gift of publicity, but you cannot bestow it unless you have it. Publicity is a two-edged sword; you can of course shun all publicity, but once you accept it and use it you cannot restrict it to favourable publicity. You have to take what you get.

The Royal Family and their advisers have lived with this problem for more than twenty years. They have tried to solve it by a policy of discreet and restrained cooperation – never pushing, but sometimes allowing themselves to be pulled. Not chasing publicity, but adapting and arranging many of their public activities to accommodate the needs of the media. Telling the press the truth and nothing but the truth, but not necessarily the whole truth. Inviting journalists to cocktails at the start of royal visits and inviting editors to the Queen's discreet informal lunches at Buckingham Palace. It may all be a great improvement on the drawbridge days of forty years ago, but none of it can guarantee a favourable press. This ensures that of all the Queen's duties and responsibilities coping with the demands of the media is the most fraught with anxiety because, if the future of the monarchy becomes an active political issue, although the decision will be taken by Parliament, the media and particularly the press are the arena where the battle will be fought. It is, after all, from the press that MPs get most of their information and most of their ideas.

It is not a purely imaginary risk, because the truth is that the British public is not irredeemably infatuated with the monarchy or the Royal Family. A minority of us are enchanted, and another probably smaller minority of us are disenchanted. Surveys suggest that you are most likely to be a supporter if you are a woman of seventy or over living in south-west England who left school at the age of fifteen; you are most likely to be an opponent if you are a young male Doctor of Philosophy in Glasgow or London. These statistical simplicities, however, mask the reality: support for and criticism of the monarchy are not divided along regional, class or age boundaries. The

OVERLEAF The press stand in the City of London for the Gulf Parade on 21 June 1991. Allocating positions for photographers is integral to the planning of any public royal event; the cameras are the eyes of the world's readers and viewers.

divisions are inside us all. Almost every individual citizen is a one-person parliament of ideas and opinions about the institution and the family that embodies it, and many of the opinions conflict. There is something in almost every British citizen that glows with pride and pleasure at the thought of the Queen and her family, and another part that bristles with suspicion. If you had to express our national attitude in a single sentence, it would be something like 'Who do they think they are and what would we do without them?'

Obviously the balance between these conflicting emotions of deference and truculence, adulation and resentment, is partly determined by the individual; but it is heavily influenced by the way the Royal Family is seen at any given time and that will depend almost entirely on the way they are presented by the media.

This is why Sunday 10 February 1991 was not a day of rest for the Queen's Press Secretary. However, when the storm had died down and the week's press cuttings were analysed in detail, it was clear that there had been virtually no direct attack on the Queen herself and little on the monarchy as an institution. The criticism was directed chiefly at the younger members of the family and, although the starting point was the accusations of frivolity and insensitivity at a time of national crisis, it broadened out to become a catalogue of all the bad publicity they had received during the past year and more. It was as if they formed a sort of bodyguard, absorbing the blows and thrusts of the enemy in order to protect the Queen. This was certainly not deliberate, but that does not make their role any less useful. If the media are to express from time to time the public's suspicions of royal influence and resentment of royal privilege, it is probably better for the monarchy that there should be some targets other than the Queen for them to aim their shafts at. After all, even a fairy story needs its wicked fairy. This does not mean, though, that everyone can relax when the dust has settled. The attacks are a warning that, underneath all the public adulation, the British capacity for suspicion and resentment of the Royal Family is still alive and capable of being aroused with surprising speed.

The Queen receives a summary of all press references to the Royal Family in the national media every morning, and the question of how much notice to take of press criticism is one that the Palace press staff and private offices have to answer every day of the year. The policy of not denying fictitious stories or seeking redress for libel through the courts encourages in the media

The Queen in consultation with her Private Secretary, Sir Robert Fellowes, in the gardens of Balmoral in September 1991. She may have free time, but she is never off duty.

a creative and imaginative approach to royal events (and non-events). There are invented stories, baseless speculation, and articles which proceed from inaccurate facts through illogical arguments to unjustifiable conclusions on which they base unworkable proposals. The objectives of the press and the Palace are not the same: the press want novelty, drama and public controversy, while the Royal Family want stability, peace and harmony. William Randolph Hearst, the American press baron, said that news was what someone somewhere didn't want printed – everything else was advertising. To the press, the best royal news is the news the Royal Family does not want printed.

It may be tempting to blame outbreaks of royal unpopularity on the media, but it is like killing the messenger. The media may at times be intrusive, inaccurate and irresponsible. They may be ill-informed and ill-disposed. But they are nevertheles the imperfect mechanism used by democracies to express the sum of the conflicting interests, ideas and emotions of the public and to strike some sort of balance between them. Sir Bernard Ingham, Mrs Thatcher's Press Secretary for eleven of her eleven and a half years as Prime Minister, compared the media to an Impressionist painting: if you look closely at any one small part of it, it seems to bear no relationship to reality, but if you stand back and look at the whole picture you can see the likeness. It is not hard to point out errors of fact in articles about the Royal Family, but the truth is that the odd factual error will not damage a newspaper's circulation, especially if it makes for a better story. Circulation is lost when newspapers lose touch with the interests, concerns, beliefs, values, emotions and opinions of their readers. This means that the media may be wrong from time to time at the factual level, but they tend to be right at the emotional level. If they express suspicion, resentment or anger, they are probably reflecting the true feelings of their readers. In a way the press, and especially the tabloid press, are like the old London mob: they may have got hold of the wrong information and ideas, their demands may be impossible to put into practice and their methods may be questionable, but the feelings being expressed are a reality and it is dangerous to ignore them.

The controversy over the Queen's immunity from income tax and other direct taxes was a good example. It flourished throughout most of 1991, with newspaper leaders and features, polls, phone-ins and a Ten-Minute Rule Bill unsuccessfully introduced in the House of Commons on 3 July. The public debate was complicated by the fact that the Queen has three separate sources of wealth.

First there is her Civil List income, voted by Parliament; in 1990 it was agreed by Parliament that for the next ten years it should be £7.9 million a year. It would clearly be absurd to tax this since it is, in effect, an expense allowance from the government for state business; two-thirds of it goes in staff salaries.

Second there is the wealth that belongs to the monarchy (or the Duchy of Lancaster) rather than to the Queen personally: palaces, jewels, paintings, collections and land worth literally billions of pounds. It may be technically at the Queen's disposal, but obviously she cannot in practice sell off the crown jewels or the Leonardo drawings or Hampton Court Palace. The asset value is enormous, but only the Crown Estates and the estates of the Duchy of Lancaster produce any substantial income. The Crown Estates produced £61 million in 1990–91, and by an ancient agreement renewed at the beginning of each reign it all goes straight to the Treasury in exchange for the Civil List allowance. The income from the Duchy of Lancaster goes towards the Queen's general expenses as Queen, in addition to the specific expenses covered by the Civil List, but not towards private expenses: shoes for awayday visits, for example, but not Christmas presents for the family.

Tom Corby (Court Correspondent for the Press Association) being briefed by Charles Anson (the Queen's Press Secretary) and Geoffrey Crawford (Assistant Press Secretary) in Buckingham Palace, September 1991. Relations between the monarchy and the media are always close but not always easy.
OVERLEAF Photographers clustering round the Queen as she tours Lisbon in 1985. Controlling the press is sometimes as much of a job as controlling the crowds.

The accounts of the Duchy are audited and published in the same way as the Civil List.

If the Queen were to pay income tax, it would presumably fall only on her third source of income, her own private wealth. Its size has never been made public, which has encouraged media speculation on the grand scale. Most of the guesses are likely to be wild overestimates. Obviously the Queen is not short of a bob or two, but there is no record of astronomical sums of private money in the Windsor family. We know that when Edward VIII abdicated he was worried about money and needed the £300,000 from the sale of Sandringham and Balmoral to George VI, and we know that George VI did not find it easy to raise the cash needed to buy them. (Balmoral and Sandringham are the two private, family-owned royal residences; Balmoral costs money to keep up, but the Sandringham estate is self-financing. All the other residences – Buckingham Palace, Windsor, Holyroodhouse – belong to the Crown and not the family.) £300,000 was not a small sum in 1937 – a typical London suburban semi-detached house cost about £1,000 – but it was not a king's ransom. We know that George VI inherited £750,000 from his father, and we can assume that prudent investment over the years will have ensured that the Queen's personal wealth is now something a good deal more than comfortable – she has bought substantial properties for the Princess Royal and the Duke and Duchess of York – but she can hardly be in the same league as the Duke of Westminster or even the Sainsbury family.

Is it right for her to be exempt? Twice during her reign, in 1972 and 1990, Parliament has looked at the question of the Queen's finances and decided she should not pay income tax, although all the rest of the Royal Family pay it. If they changed their mind, then the immunity would end; it is Parliament's decision, not the Queen's. It all sounds very straightforward. But whatever may be the technical, legal and historical arguments, there is something about royal tax exemption that stirs primitive emotions in the British taxpayer's breast: a feeling of 'I pay, so why shouldn't she?', which cannot be refuted by rational argument.

Even the obsession of the media with the private lives of the Royal Family can be defended, though it creates yet another royal dilemma. It may be reasonable for company chairmen or top civil servants to say that their private lives are no business of the press, but they are not looked upon to set standards of behaviour or provide moral leadership. It is different for the sovereign. The private life of the Queen and all the Royal Family is a matter of serious public interest. The dilemma is that the only way for them to ensure privacy is to build barriers and live their private lives in a sort of information fortress, thereby becoming more and more remote and inviting criticism for being out of touch. When the eight-year-old Prince Charles started his first term at a preparatory school in Cheam in 1957, the press stake-out of the building and grounds looked as if this would make it impossible for him to be educated in a school with other children; for their sake and his it seemed he would have to be educated privately as the Queen had been, which was exactly the practice which the press were trying to reform. On that occasion the Queen put this paradox to the newspaper editors and they agreed to leave the school alone after a press open day, which solved that particular problem but did not remove the dilemma.

One of the unavoidable duties of the modern monarchy is to confront this dilemma every day. Every action of the sovereign is liable to make the headlines. This does not mean everything has to be tailored for media presentation, but it does mean that the press secretaries and advisers in the Palace have to try and foresee what the media reaction is likely to be. The action may still be taken, but it should not be taken in ignorance of its possible press repercussions.

Since the press and the monarchy both need each other, but for very different reasons, their relationship will always be close but never easy or comfortable. To those who sail the ship of state, the media are like the sea: you enjoy it and take advantage of it when it is calm, and you do your best to protect yourself from it when it is rough, but you never try to fool yourself that you can control it. And you cannot afford to be so busy coping with the waves that you do not notice a change in the tide.

10

FORTY YEARS ON

It is not too difficult to describe what the monarchy does, but a list of a year's activities does not add up to an answer to the questions of what the monarchy is and what it is for. The Queen is the present monarch, but the monarchy existed for 1,000 years before she came to the throne. It may carry on for another 1,000 years or it may come to an end very soon. So what is it?

Ultimately the monarchy is an institution, in the sense that Eton, Gray's Inn, the Bank of England, the House of Commons, the Transport and General Workers' Union, and ICI are institutions. An institution is a group of people, usually in a particular place and often in a specific set of buildings, who discharge a function and preserve and update a body of knowledge and a code of practice; they pass these on to their successors so that the institution, the service it performs, the values it embodies, the practices it encourages and the standards it sets may outlive its present members and continue down the generations and the centuries. They have no guarantee of immortality – every year sees the death of some

ABOVE The Queen and Prince Philip on board HMY *Britannia* in Miami, Florida, during the state visit to the USA in May 1991. For forty years the Queen has represented and symbolized Britain for the rest of the world.

The Queen aged three with her parents, who were then the Duke
and Duchess of York. Since her father had an older brother, the
future Edward VIII, who succeeded and abdicated in 1936, no one
expected her to become sovereign.

old institutions and the birth of new ones – but they offer as much permanence
as human societies can construct in a mutable and mortal world. They are
the building blocks of civilizations.

So, if the monarchy is an institution, what is it for? Or, to be more specific,
what services does Britain's constitutional monarchy provide that other forms
of government do not provide or provide in a different way? The formal,

The Queen with Prince Charles shortly after he was born on 14
November 1948. Unlike his mother, the Prince was heir apparent
to the throne from the age of three, when his grandfather George VI
died. The Queen was only ever heir presumptive since, in theory,
George VI could have produced a male heir to displace her in the
line of succession.

OPPOSITE Princess Anne's christening, Buckingham Palace,
October 1950. On the Queen's left is the Queen Mother and on
her right her grandmother Queen Mary (1867–1953), widow of
George V. The four generations illustrate the continuity of the
British monarchy.

official functions are well established: the sovereign is Head of State, Head of the judiciary, Head of the Church of England, Head of the armed services, and Head of the Commonwealth. She is the source of political legitimacy at home and the representative of Britain to the rest of the world. The informal, unofficial services are, however, not so well codified or widely recognized. They have been touched on during the course of this book, but it might be helpful to summarize them here.

CONSTITUTIONAL ARBITRATION In times of crisis, as with hung parliaments, the lack of an automatic choice of prime minister or an unjustifiable and unnecessary request for a dissolution of Parliament, the monarchy provides an impartial and non-political arbitrator, like an umpire called in when the players cannot agree. It would also be able to intervene if the government acted unconstitutionally by, say, putting the opposition in jail, abolishing elections or instructing the police not to prosecute members of the government for criminal offences.

STABILITY A form of government that only came into being yesterday can quite easily be overthrown tomorrow; an institution sanctified by 1,000 years of sovereignty is more deeply embedded in the consciousness of the nation and more closely woven into the fabric of political life. It can still be overthrown (and was by Oliver Cromwell in 1649), but people are likely to think very hard before they pick up the sword.

CONTINUITY Governments come and go. A week is a long time in Parliament and five years is a lifetime. But the sovereign is always there, and the apparatus of monarchy helps to bridge the discontinuities of party politics.

EXPERIENCE A lifetime of reading state papers, meeting heads of state and ambassadors, and holding a weekly audience with the Prime Minister gives the Queen an unequalled store of knowledge

The first twenty years: the Queen with her family in 1972, the twentieth year of her reign. Whereas party politics represents public life as a battlefield, the monarchy presents it as a family circle.

and experience. Politicians see state papers only when they are in office, but the Queen sees them every day. Her constitutional right to be consulted, to encourage and to warn makes this experience available to every government.

UNITY Party politics is about disagreement and confrontation. It encourages polarization – rich against poor, north against south, management against unions, black against white, Catholic against Protestant. Parliament institutionalizes division and conflict. The monarchy is about national unity and institutionalizes cooperation and consensus.

SUCCESSION The hereditary principle does more than provide a formula for unopposed succession. It also means that everyone knows who the successor is likely to be, and that he or she will have been groomed for the job from birth.

INTELLIGIBILITY A family at the head of a nation's affairs is something everyone can understand and identify with. It makes the state seem human, personal and accessible. Parliament portrays public life as a battlefield; the monarchy portrays it as a family circle.

RECOGNITION OF ACHIEVEMENT By honours, awards, visits, patronage and sponsorship the sovereign and the Royal Family can recognize and reward achievement by individuals and organizations, and publicly affirm their value to the nation.

FOCUS OF ALLEGIANCE A person and a family are a powerful symbol for the armed services of what they are fighting for, and are not so vulnerable to the winds of political favour in supporting the forces and honouring their sacrifice.

MORAL LEADERSHIP Because the monarchy is permanent, it can set a consistent moral standard which people can look to as a guide and example.

MODEL OF BEHAVIOUR The monarchy can also give the nation an example or, to be more precise, a range of examples of acceptable behaviour in the smaller matters of social convention and behaviour. Even when some members of the Royal Family do not behave

The Queen Mother between her two daughters taking a photo-
break from a family celebration of her ninetieth birthday. Her
nuclear family of the 1930s is on its way to becoming a dynasty. The
Queen now has ten direct living descendants; there are some 200
living descendants of Queen Victoria, all in direct line to the throne.

as well as people expect them to, they are still contributing to the
process of reviewing and revising the nation's behaviour patterns.

CUSTODIANSHIP OF THE PAST Through its ceremony, pageantry
and ritual the monarchy preserves the link with Britain's history
and reminds people of the country's past achievements and the
antiquity of their state.

TRUSTEESHIP OF THE FUTURE By being close to the heart of affairs, but outside the political arena, the Royal Family can focus attention on the country's long-term dangers and opportunities as a counterweight to the inevitably short-term preoccupations of politicians in the heat of the party battle.

UNITING THE NATION WITH THE STATE Most important of all is the combination of the constitutional role as Head of the State and the social role as Head of the Nation within a single institution, a single family and a single office. If the sovereign can be the focus of the people's loyalty, pride, patriotism and sense of nationhood, then the people are simultaneously focusing these emotions on the State of which the Queen is the constitutional head; they are confirming and supporting the legitimacy of the political, legal and economic system which regulates their daily lives.

These functions of the British monarchy are of a different order from the constitutional duties such as opening and dissolving Parliament, approving Orders in Council, creating peers, sending for new prime ministers and signing Acts of Parliament. Some of the functions are part of any system of hereditary monarchy, but others are very much in the hands of the sovereign; they can be done well, or adequately, or badly, or not done at all. They are the ones concerned with behaviour, values and standards; the ones which make the Queen into the accepted Head of the Nation; the ones which earn the respect, loyalty and pride of the people so that they feel she belongs to them, that she is 'our Queen'. If for whatever reason that feeling dies out, if the sovereign becomes just another occupant of a high office of state with no more relevance to people's daily lives and inner feelings than the Lord Chief Justice or the Governor of the Bank of England, then that crucial link between nation and state will be seriously weakened and will perhaps break.

OPPOSITE Forty-two-year-old Prince Charles talking to fellow Knights of the Thistle after the procession in Edinburgh on 2 July 1991. Ever since his birth he has been groomed for the job of King. OVERLEAF Prince Henry in a carriage at the Trooping the Colour ceremony in June 1991. If the fates are kind and the British people still want a monarchy, his brother William could be on the throne in the second half of the next century.

FINANCIAL RECTITUDE This includes not just sharp business practice but also any suggestion of using membership of the Royal Family for personal gain, as when it was reported that the Duchess of York was personally keeping the royalties on *Budgie the Little Helicopter*, her children's book that was published in September 1989.

CONSPICUOUS THRIFT By some curious paradox the British seem to be in favour of splendour, but against extravagance. We want 'our Queen' to be decked in gold and jewels and ride in a fairytale coach drawn by white horses, but we want her to be careful with 'our money' – no waste, self-indulgence or lavish expenditure for personal enjoyment.

MORAL PROPRIETY The Royal Family are expected to be several steps behind the times. Even though attitudes to things like drugs, pornography, infidelity and homosexual relationships are much more relaxed and permissive than they were in 1952, the licence does not extend to representatives of the monarchy.

EMOTIONAL SENSITIVITY Royalty are expected to catch and share the national mood. In terms of strict protocol it would be normal for the Queen to be 'represented' at the memorial service for victims of the Lockerbie air crash, but there was widespread feeling that she or at least a senior member of the family should have attended in person.

ATTENDANCE TO DUTY Perhaps as a result of receiving money from the taxpayer, the Royal Family are expected to earn their keep by attendance at public functions. From time to time the press spot that some member of the family has not been pulling their weight and make a fuss about it.

AVOIDANCE OF CONTROVERSY Constitutionally the sovereign is not allowed to speak in public on serious matters without the agreement of ministers, but this applies only to the sovereign. The Prince of Wales has shown, as the Duke of Edinburgh did before him, that it is possible, even if risky, for other members of the Royal Family to express in public an opinion which may provoke disagreement. Nevertheless the topic has to be chosen with care

The Duke of Edinburgh, beside the Queen, returns the salute at the
Gulf Parade march past. One of the characteristics of the Royal
Family is to share in moments of high national emotion.

BELOW National patriotic emotion broke out in street parties all
over Britain at the time of the Queen's Silver Jubilee in 1977.
Loyalty to the Queen as Head of the Nation brings with it a feeling
of national unity and identity, and an acceptance of the legitimacy
and authority of the state of which she is also the head.
OPPOSITE One family in London left their neighbours in no doubt
about the strength of their loyalty and affection at the time of the
Queen's Silver Jubilee in 1977.

and must not be one which will favour one of the political parties or upset a significant proportion of the general public. In the early 1960s, for example, it was not possible for them to be personally identified with blood sports.

DOMESTIC VIRTUE The British people look to the Royal Family as a model of family behaviour. They expect husbands and wives to be together whenever they can, although they do not expect extravagant displays of emotion in public. They expect mothers to be with their children and bring them up personally, and not to subcontract that responsibility to nannies. In practice of course it is illogical to expect the Royal Family to carry out all their public duties without having someone to look after the children, but public expectations are not bound by logic and practicality. When royal behaviour differs from their own, people have to decide whether there is something wrong with themselves or something wrong with the Royal Family. Fashions change, of course. There was no objection in the 1930s when the Queen and Princess Margaret were educated privately at home by a governess, but by the 1950s people would have felt it wrong for the Queen's children not to be educated in schools like everyone else.

SUBMISSION TO THE LAW 'Be you never so high, the law is above you.' The slightest suspicion that members of the Royal Family may be using their position to get away with even small misdemeanours like speeding offences causes immediate public outcry.

POLITENESS AND AFFABILITY By another paradox the Royal Family are expected to be royal, but not to act as if they were royal. Any hint of upper-class arrogance by younger members of the family is an immediate cue for press attacks. Discourtesies like arriving late, being rude, snobbish, patronizing or visibly bored are taken not as personal failings but as a national affront.

While these may be the most sensitive areas, they cannot amount to a complete code of conduct for the Queen or the Royal Family. It is not something you can do by numbers or by following a drill or a set of instructions. In the end the job of the sovereign is to embody, personify and

The Queen in conversation with Sir Roger Tomkys, British
ambassador to Kenya, following his knighthood at Buckingham
Palace in June 1991.

personalize the nation's identity. It is impossible to list all the separate
components of that abstract idea, but when we feel British and not, for
example, American, what do we mean beyond the documentary proof that
we are legally British citizens? Whatever complex blend of ideas and emotions
may lie behind that feeling, there can be no doubt that for the vast majority
of the British people it is the Queen, the Royal Family and the monarchy
which give it visible and comprehensible form.

The job of sovereign is a strange one if you try to look at it objectively. It offers a level of wealth, comfort, prestige, influence and job security beyond most people's imagination. There is no job description, there are no formal qualifications, there is no entrance examination or selection interview. You have no boss. It is, however, governed by a series of restrictions and obligations from which you are never free and, if you neglect them, you put at hazard not just yourself and your family but an institution which has lasted for over a millennium. This means that, when it comes to the crunch, you always have to put the demands of the job above personal wishes; from the point of view of the monarchy, Edward VIII's great betrayal was to put his own wishes first. The Queen has now been doing this job for forty years. Few people do a single job for so long, and even fewer without possibility of promotion or prospect of retirement. You cannot give it up at sixty-five and retire to a bungalow in Budleigh Salterton. You can have spare time, but you can never be off duty. On any day of your life you can let down fifty-seven million people, perhaps 100 million if you include the sovereign's Commonwealth subjects. And although there are many jobs to be done, the final measurement of success does not depend simply on how efficiently you do them. The Queen has said that her role is not doing, but being. In the end it is not what you do, but what you are – and what you know you will have to be for the whole of your life.

ILLUSTRATION SOURCES

The majority of the photographs in this book are by David Secombe. We are grateful to the following for the remainder:

CAMERA PRESS pages 6, 7 (Baron), 11 (Richard Open), 14 (Richard Open), 19, 25 (John Drysdale), 26–27, 66 (Stewart Mark), 92 (Lionel Cherruault), 121, 149 (Malcolm Sanderton), 151, 153, 154 (Mark Stewart), 177, 188 (Imperial War Museum), 217 (Marcus Adams), 218 (Baron), 219 (Cecil Beaton), 221 (Patrick Lichfield), 226–227, 232 (Fritz Curzon)

LIONEL CHERRUAULT pages 212–213

ANDREA CRINGEAN/BBC COPYRIGHT page 145 above

TIM GRAHAM pages 10, 20–21, 40–41, 86, 88–89, 98–99, 129, 133, 150, 166–177, 196, 203, 223, 233

IMPACT page 164 (Philippe Achache)

JS LIBRARY INTERNATIONAL page 114

PRESS ASSOCIATION page 23

REX FEATURES pages 12–13 (Peter Brooker), 187 (*Sun*)

FRANK SPOONER PICTURES pages 96 and 97 (Chris Sattleberger/Gamma), 100 (Pono Presse/Gamma)

TOPHAM pages 47 (Associated Press), 62, 144, 197 (Associated Press)

UNIVERSAL PICTORIAL PRESS page 43

INDEX

Page numbers in *italic* refer to the illustrations and captions